MW00954589

Rooting Up:
Essays in Modern Branding

By Emily Soccorsy and Justin Foster

RIGHTEOUS BAR FIGHT LLC. Copyright © **2019** by Emily Soccorsy and Justin Foster. All rights reserved. Printed in the United States of America. No part of this book may be used or reproduced in any manner whatsoever without written permission.

TABLE OF CONTENTS

DEDICATION

To our families - both in blood and in spirit.

INTRODUCTION

It's basically impossible to know when you start something where you will end up.

In late 2014, it became apparent to both of us that we were going to start something. The realization of what that something was came quickly after. Blending our ideas on branding, our experience in and with leadership, and our expertise as storytellers with the lack of grounded, realistic methods of marketing available to businesses, and the absence of wise, measured marketing guidance, it became clear that we were going to start a non-agency. We used that term from the get-go. In our minds, a non-agency meant our baby endeavor wasn't going to be a traditional branding agency, offering every marketing-related service under the sun.

It was not going to charge clients big markups to ensure a profit margin. It would not manage the high cost of significant overhead to keep a modern, hip office and to maintain and promote its own image of greatness. It was not going to employ dozens of people (and rapidly lay them off after losing big clients) and it would not offer clients quick-fixes and gasp-inducing, smoke-and-mirrors brand reveal experiences. And we were not going to walk around wearing black turtlenecks surrounded by interns we treated like crap.

Justin had started and run agencies and had experienced the painful pitfalls – high turnover, building client dependency, the stress of keeping up appearances, and the endless pivots between what a client really needed and what you needed to sell to keep the doors open. Emily had worked with and in multiple agencies and had experienced the bluster and seen the human cost. The something we were building wasn't going to be a consulting business, either. That would not work because our passion was around being collaborative and long-term; not prescriptive and brief as many consultants tend to be.

Starting a non-agency was such an obvious decision, well before we began, it almost seemed like a forgone conclusion.

It was blatant to us, even then, that great change was coming to the established ways of thinking about marketing and branding. Simon Sinek's uber-popular "Start with Why" TED talk premiered March 2014 and in our minds, his ideas marked the trailhead for a whole new era for how organizations shared their message with the world.

At the same time, we saw and experienced that moment as a return to ancient principles of tradition sharing, storytelling and inspiration. We wanted to create a ragtag band of sovereign people dedicated to charting the rest of the course, and open to collaborating with us. We were going to create something that didn't exist. We were going to fashion a business our former corporate selves could never be and our former agency selves didn't have the permission to build.

The first time trying our crazy ideas in an actual client session came in late 2014 in Dallas, Texas. A friend of Justin's had become the head of sales for an industrial fan company, and they needed a brand strategy, message and a marketing plan. Justin asked Emily if she wanted to do the project together. She agreed without hesitation – despite already being gainfully employed and without too much clarity on how the session would unfold. Although we had solid ideas and methods, this would be the first time we blended our facilitation, our ideas and our abilities for the benefit of a client. (This strategic day would later become known as a Root Session.)

All entrepreneurial ventures are really just acts of faith. While we didn't know much about how it would ultimately turn out, we had faith in our intellect and experience. We had faith about our approach and how we had blended our styles for the good of other people we had advised and worked for. We had faith that the alchemy, although not full formed, was gold waiting to be mined. We had faith that Bill, the founder of the industrial fan company, had made the right decision to engage with us.

In a spartan conference room in a Quality Inn in Grapevine, Texas, magic ensued. The session unfolded with a viscosity only creative energy can produce. Emily began sketching words and images about the session in one of her many sketch pads. At the end of the day, Bill was in tears and made the proclamation, "if I would have known how great this would be, I would have paid you 10 times your fee." The shedding of tears and the easy surrender of treasure are both signs of something cosmic in action. After the session, we got in the rental car and sat for a moment, taking in the magic of the day. "What was that?" one of us asked. "I don't know. But let's do it again!" was the resounding answer.

Over the next year, we practiced our craft and honed our methods. In that time, we took on everything with obsessive intention, meticulous detail and soulful alignment. We constantly asked for feedback and changed before, during, and after every engagement. After scads of planning, testing, adjusting (and more than a lot of arguing and discussion), Root + River was born.

When we officially launched in January 2016, we were aware we weren't really launching a business. We were creating a movement. We had established a platform, not really for us, but for all who wanted to brand differently and needed the support, the provocation and the method to do so.

Little did we know that nearly four years into this endeavor, we would have directly guided the brand strategy of more than a hundred companies, profoundly touched hundreds of lives through coaching and mentoring, and reached the ears, hearts and minds of the thousands of people we have shared this heart-based approach to branding with.

In every instance, we have been affirmed in our work by the results people share with us: growing businesses, healthy internal cultures, a sense of relief and joy in their work, uncovering deeper meaning in what they do, a renewed sense of hope, and an inspiration to work from their souls.

Our goal from the outset was not to form a business to make money. It was to create an endeavor that would change the way people thought. Despite scads of dissent between us along the way, we always agreed that our primary objective, in every engagement, in every speaking opportunity, in every coaching relationship, was to break the way people thought about branding. It was to return people to their own true decision center – their inner intuition. It was to inspire leaders to go inward.

While we are most proud of the team we have built around us to make that happen, our next greatest achievement is the way our work has led people back to themselves.

This is a movement. It is a movement about an approach we call intrinsic branding – building brands from the inside out. It is designed to end the 20th century obsession companies had with building brands in reverse – from the outside in. This movement is driven by ending the manufactured reality-style of branding that the propaganda machines, ad agencies and mass media created beginning in the late 1940s, and persisted through the 50s, 60s and into the 1990s. In the post-war era, branding was mainly driven by creating an idyllic perception around a brand name, a product or a service and emotionally coercing and manipulating the audience into believing that possessing that product or adhering to that venerated appearance gave them the holy grail of modern society: acceptance and assimilation.

Along with the many excruciating lessons of the second World War, one was that standing out could get you – and your family – incarcerated or killed. With a public sensitive to the danger in standing out, and with mass media suddenly available with a broad new scale, marketers of the time pitched fitting in.

For decades, it seemed to work.

The trouble was the ideal. Whether imagined as Betty Crockers, or Marlboro men, businesses became accustomed to having an image that represented what they sold as a fiction, a construct. While these carefully staged and curated images were compelling visually and emotionally, and successfully embodied ideals of the age (perfect, convenient housewifery and rugged, independent and expansive man on the range), they were disconnected from the products themselves and completely detached from the foundations of the companies that sold them.

As it turned out, consuming processed food and refined sugars and tobacco are not necessarily as bold, or noble, as the images used to sell them were. And these campaigns revealed nothing about the ethics of the massive organizations that sold them to the American public. Opinions of big tobacco or processed food manufacturers aside, in the 21st century, this sort of disconnect and manipulative distraction is not a tenable strategy. It will, at some point, be revealed.

With the introduction of total visibility into corporations that once hid behind an opaque curtain, companies that advertise one thing and then behave in polar opposite ways will be exposed. Leaders who endorse these campaigns of distraction (at best) or misrepresentation (at worst) and then create hostile environments, treat their employees poorly or behave outside the bounds of societal acceptance, will be rejected right out of their chief executive positions. The gap that used to be the shangri-la for advertisers has now become a dangerous liability, thanks to the advent of the internet, and sites like Glassdoor.com, and so many others.

Root + River does not exist to expose people, but to recognize that when we create gaps, for whatever reason, we are adding stress to ourselves, to our partners, and adding risk to our businesses. We exist to spur us as a society to think deeper about the meaning of our work, to become invested in that meaning and then to courageously and confidently convey that with truth and clarity.

From the beginning of our creative venture, our convictions first emerged in the form of posts and articles, a collection that you are reading here. As we continued to articulate, share and pontificate, we began to codify and polish our core tenets, beliefs and ideas. This culminated in a core philosophy on branding and marketing that is timeless and expressed in these mantras:

- A great brand is a spiritual experience.
- Strategy before tactics. Always.
- Brand and business model must be in alignment.
- Branding is everyone's role.
- To be the best at marketing, outsource specialized tasks.
- Marketing output can't suck - but don't overpay for it.
- Pay for retention not attention.
- Boredom is the enemy of brand; assholes are the enemy of culture.

These principles are woven into what you will be reading here; sometimes with an obvious flavor of defiance, or with the more subtle flavor of beauty – but always the flavor of love.

You will see us find and refine our voice. You will see us consciously blend our ideas so that our content contained the symmetry of our partnership. We've chosen not to go back and edit out the signs of our evolution into what we are today: a kinder, gentler and more accepting Root + River. We think you have the intelligence to see our steady progress to become more of who we are.

These essays are grouped into three categories:

Branding Birds & Bees:
Most of us have a static knowledge set on branding and marketing. The essays in this section take you back to the basics of intrinsic branding, without the uncomfortable visit from mom or dad.

Leading is Branding:
A brand is how other people experience what you believe and how you behave. Whether you are a solo entrepreneur or a corporate executive, the brand (yours and the organization) is directly impacted by the style of your leadership.

New World Marketing:
The old world of target audiences, demographics and ad campaigns is done. The new world of connecting to the heart, taking a stand and spurring word of mouth is at hand. This section gives you some insight on navigating in this new world.

Our mission is to inspire leaders to go inward. If these readings stirred your soul, please reach out to us! Send us an email from our website (rootandriver.com), follow us on social media or attend one of our BrandLabs. If you know of any other defiant entrepreneurs or marketers who want to use their brands to change the world, please share this book with them.

With gratitude,
Emily + Justin

SECTION 1:
Branding Birds + Bees

KNOW THYSELF: A 21ST CENTURY BRANDING PRINCIPLE

One of the most surprising moments of a Root Session is when our beloved client has the realization their brand was already inside of them. We did not tell them what their brand is. They discover it.

How is this possible?

It's been taught that branding is an external thing. Something you want to be, some construct you build, one aspirational and slightly delusional brick at a time. The Marlboro man, Betty Crocker, Tony the Tiger ... and that local car dealership owner who yells at the television camera.

While there certainly is an external component to brand, a brand exists inside of you — and inside of your organization. Or more specifically, a brand exists inside of each human who touches your brand. And it's always been this way.

We call what we do **intrinsic branding**. This is not some new age-y, touchy-feely way of saying we do marketing. Intrinsic branding is the direct descendant of ancient principles being brought back to life due to massive shifts in society and business.

Know thyself.

This statement, chiseled into the stone courtyard of the Temple of Apollo at Delphi in 500 B.C., is one of the world's oldest philosophical directives. Socrates used the concept as a basis for his teachings, evolving it into the missive that an unexamined life is not worth living. Plato continued to encourage people to go inward and claimed the essence of all knowledge is self-knowledge.

Over time, it has been the examination of life (our feelings, our experiences, our failures and hopes, our victories and successes, our empires and revolutions) that has informed and conveyed the crafts of oral tradition, art, poetry, plays, books, performance art, visual creation, journalism and advertising, communication, technology and virtual reality — as well as our business endeavors.

If the unexamined life is not worth living, can the unexamined mission, endeavor or movement be worth an investment of time and resources?

We posit it cannot.

A contemporary brand example: Patagonia.

This legendary outdoor gear manufacturer certainly knows themselves. Like many intrinsically driven ventures, Patagonia founder Yvon Chouinard just wanted some mountain climbing gear that didn't suck. So he started a company that was deeply rooted in his core beliefs. Chouinard and his team implemented many ideas that would seem counter to good business sense. They tell their customers to think twice before buying. They have a lifetime guarantee that is rigorously upheld. They don't set profit goals ("We let our customers tell us how much money we're going to make," said

Chouinard recently.) They tell their employees Patagonia's philosophies are not rules; they are guidelines.

More recently, they used their brand equity to vocally and vigorously challenge President Trump's proposed reduction in size of the Bear Ears National Monument in Utah — running a series of ads that state, "The President Stole Your Land." Chouinard himself, when invited to testify in front of the House Committee on Natural Resources, refused to do so and recommended the Chairman and the President refer to their public statements about the theft of public lands from the public. By sticking to their principles and high standards, Patagonia continues to grow as a brand and as a business (it has tripled profits since 2008).

Brands and leaders who don't know themselves tend to drift away from stated values every time the market shifts or a competitor does something aggressive. They tend to be much more extrinsic about their brand – obsessed with image and message control – yet insecure and wishy-washy about taking a stand. Just like a person who doesn't know themselves, these brands chase acceptance and approval from their audiences.

BRANDING HAPPENS IN MOMENTS

A brand doesn't magically appear.

A logo might. But not a brand. Brands are really deeply seeded ideas, so they take time to formulate completely, mature and bear fruit.

Brands are made, not in a moment, but in moments — big and small.

Where do these moments arise from? How do we tend to them? Just like in life, many of them are unplanned.

Have you ever considered what your brand moments are?

Not sure?

Anytime people interact your with brand is a brand moment. Anytime you talk about your brand or business with someone who has not heard about it before is a brand moment. Hiring and onboarding a new person to your team is a brand moment. Speaking in front of a larger audience than would fit in front of your desk is a brand moment.

When is your next conversation about your business?

Are you hiring someone this year?

Do you have any plans to speak to a group this year?

In any of these scenarios, are you clear on what you will share? Do you know how you will express your brand?

Our client and friend Mike O'Krent had a big moment in 2018 during his TedX talk, one in which we were honored to help him prepare for.

A business owner his entire life, Mike didn't take this opportunity to speak about his business, to pitch people to buy crap or to boast about his success. Instead, Mike chose to speak about the ideas that move him, and the emotionally poignant moments in his life, the ones that choke him up and give him great joy. He chose to share the ideas that inform the soulful work he has chosen to do in various manifestations throughout his career.

Great brands always stay in the idea business.

Sure, they market their products and services. But they also leave plenty of space for ideas to emerge from themselves, their team and their clients. They know the ideas produce the products, which is why they put ideas higher on the priority hierarchy that products.

So again, how do you tend to these ideas, these moments?

We say, prepare for the unplanned and plan for the planned.

Language matters. What you say about your brand, the words you carefully select, and how you feel about them, have the most impact on how your message will be received. Period. If you feel unclear or insecure about how you talk about your brand, your audience will feel insecurity and lack of clarity.

Take time. Again, branding is a practice. It takes time to cultivate and does not spontaneously come out of your mouth. It takes consideration, noticing, practice and refinement. If you are serious about developing your brand, set aside time this year to do this work.

Salesforce founder and CEO Marc Benioff unplugged for two weeks in 2018. And from that came a flood of revelations, new ideas and new moments. The lesson? Many moments don't come from working harder. They come from the pause; the liminal moment between things that produce even more moments. These pauses usually don't happen on their own. We must make them happen.

Make a plan. If you do not commit yourself to speak about your brand this year to a larger audience (a group of five or more people counts), you will not do it. If you are serious about building your brand, sign yourself up to talk to a mastermind group, to a gathering of contemporaries, or to a local business organization. Put this planned moment on the calendar. Then work toward it.

Get an outside perspective. Listen, we know we might seem self-serving by advocating this, but the reality is you cannot brand in a vacuum. What sounds good in your muddy, muddy mind will, 9,999 out of 10,000 times, fall flat in the eardrums — and heart– of another human. Seek outside counsel on your brand.

Finally, and most importantly, commit to the long game of branding. The best things in life and in business take time, and pacing, to fully manifest and to fully enjoy.

In our insanely paced culture, this is a countercultural idea: slow down. Be steady and consistent. Expect results to blossom over time.

If you do, the moments — planned and unplanned — won't pass you by.

IN MODERN BRANDING, PERCEPTION IS NO LONGER REALITY

Some of the strongest branding advice we give to clients is this: when building a brand don't add more pretense.

You may nod your head at this idea, feel moved to hit Like or Share, or to share with your friend in marketing, but are you too comfortable, too clad in precious pretense, to take a full-frontal look at what that means for you? And for the brand(s) you represent?

Do you extol the virtues of being "real" while being sure every photo you ever post of your company or of yourself is perfectly framed, filtered and fixed?

Do you accept that "knowing your why" is important, then avoid trying to determine it and just run Facebook ads instead?

Consider.

Branding has always been about perception.

But it's only in the last five years the idea of branding has evolved. Now branding is about having your perception align with and accurately reflect the reality of you, of your organization, in total. That means mess-ups and magnificence, stellar IPOs and failed ventures. All of it.

All of this reality makes up your brand. Ask Wells Fargo. Or GM. Or Uber.

Perfection is a myth. Worse than that, our belief in perfection creates a cancer inside of us, and inside of our organizations.

Perfectionism also creates a lot of bad leadership habits. Mostly because it brings shame to simply being human. We humans are messy. We make mistakes. We fail. All of this becomes part of your brand story when you let go of the perfection bar as a standard form of measurement.

The idea of perfection is notoriously set in motion through propagandizing. This command-and-control approach obsessively seeks to craft the narrative and spin the message. But in this hyper-connected world, building a brand off of this kind of primping and polishing is not sustainable. Over time, it makes you look desperate and out of touch.

Here are a few specific tips to consider:

> **Truth is the best brand strategy.** This starts with a leadership team that knows what they stand for and consistently holds to a set of beliefs and values, even under great pressure. When you have a leadership team that practices what they preach, you don't have as much worry about public perception.

> **The story is in the mess.** When you live out your brand in a real and raw way, you are inviting people to your story. When you hide the messiness of being human, you hide all of the interesting aspects of your story.

Innovation comes from failure. Want to build a brand as an innovator? Then be public about your failures. The Wright Brothers, Thomas Edison, JetBlue, 3M, NASA and Google all built brands by embracing failure as part of the journey to innovation.

So, the choice is yours as leader. You can continue to give lip service to the idea of having a purpose-driven brand while still trying to be the most popular person at the party.

Or, dig in to yourself and your brand to truly understand what the most important thing is that you need to convey to the world. Being real isn't about giving you permission to puke your life out to the world. Rather, it gives you the opportunity to find the most significant of your ideas and share that — vulnerabilities and victories — because if you don't, it will eat you alive.

If you do share that truth, it may just change the world. For real.

WHY IS MARKETING SO OVERWHELMING?

Yes, it is. Also, no, it's not. Here's when marketing is overwhelming:

When you have an industrial-age mindset about marketing – all linear processes and box checking. Reality: You will never be able to check all the marketing boxes. Ever. There are now way too many of them.

When you are looking to buy a solution to your "marketing problem." Most marketing companies are making loads of money selling solutions to problems that don't really exist. You know this deep down. So why do you keep buying them, listening and taking their calls?

If you have low self-worth, you attract people who want to take advantage of your fear, uncertainty and doubt (we call this FUD). Consider this: how often is the pitch from the marketing company about being left out, left behind or becoming obsolete?

Marketing is no longer overwhelming when you put strategy first and tactics second. This means your brand and business strategies are in alignment first before you decide the best tactics and tools to implement those strategies.

In addition, marketing becomes less overwhelming when:

You understand your mission in your life and work. Your mission becomes a test for all business decisions. If it doesn't fit your mission, you say no! As we frequently say, you build a career by saying yes, you build a brand by saying no.

You have a message you can't wait to share. A clear, convincing message helps you determine the marketing tools that will most effectively amplify this message.

You understand and embrace the dynamics of 21st century business and how they are different from the 20th century way of doing business.

You organize your branding and marketing practices around the three most proven contemporary methods: 1) Building relationships 2) Telling stories through content and 3) Creating memorable experiences. If you do these three things, you will see that most "marketing solutions" are neither marketing nor solutions.

To answer the question, what you should avoid doing? Anything not rooted in your mission — the thing you are here to accomplish that only you can do. This is the essence of our work of intrinsic branding – to find this place in you and help you make it a vibrant, profitable brand.

Avoid anything that makes your stomach turn a bit or triggers your B.S. sensor.

Avoid any marketing tactic (not matter how shiny!) that you would not like used on you.

Here's what you should do: commit to a practice of branding and marketing that feels most natural to you — it's the only thing that you will be able to sustain. And marketing today needs to be consistent. And if marketing ever becomes overwhelming, check your clarity, convictions and courage. These are the best tools for avoiding overwhelm — both in life or in business!

WHO THE HECK IS MY TARGET MARKET?

Let's start with this bit of heresy: there are no target markets.

One reason is practical: traditional demographics have broken audiences into chunks, which have been shattered into even smaller groups based on granular data we now have on nearly any organizable group. So, there's no one singular market to target.

The other reason is ethical: no one wants to be anyone's target. To call a group of humans a "target market" dehumanizes them and reduces them to a set of stats and labels.

If you allow yourself to lay back into the soft folds of the idea that a target market exists, anxiously waiting to hear about whatever you are selling, you lose the chance to understand why your offering matters. And why any other human being would find it appealing or necessary or of value.

We much prefer to reframe the question this way:

Who is the one person you are trying to reach?

Stop for a second and consider. If you could only make a very deep impact on one person in your life's work (and this is much more realistic for most of us than the delusion we are going to touch millions) — who would that person be? What would they be wrestling with now? Where are they — in their career, in their home life, in their own life's work?

- What do they care about?
- What do they fear?
- What do they see?
- What are they seeking?

You can see this approach requires you to dig way deeper than surface demographics, drilling down into their soul.

Over the last several years of working together, and walking alongside clients during their brand discovery process and in Root Sessions, we've been on this journey more than 100 times.

There is no exact equation for discovering your one person, your ideal audience. By its very nature, this approach is individualistic, intuitive and highly contextual to each brand. That said, there are some common alchemy ingredients we can share:

- Common values – They believe what you believe.
- Shared suffering – They have experienced the same struggles and trials you have.
- Similar POV – They see the world as you do.

In our work of intrinsic branding, we help you deeply understand this individual, and then begin to speak to this person using the message you believe at your root. As you articulate it, and become a master of your brand conversation, sharing your message with the world, there are real, tangible benefits.

You will attract people that match your ideal audience, and they will reach out to you. (If you call them leads, that's fine; we call them tribe.)

The people you attract will have completed 50-70% of the sales or vetting process before you even speak. (Statistics range but a well-regarded Forrester study puts this number at 67%).

You will have richer conversations, deeper relationships and enjoy a more rapid connection with other humans who meet your criteria faster than if you had not.

You will repel those who don't get it and who don't respect your value.

You will create an army of followers and fans who say nice things about you – for free!

The biggest change when you shift to this way of thinking is that you will begin to look into the eyes of every person you meet, seeking that spark that says,

"Ah. There you are! I've been waiting for you."

HOW DO I MONETIZE MY TALENTS?

Despite what many believed when we began our company, we are not nutty spiritualists waiting for the clouds to part and money to fall like a tender rain.

We are unabashed capitalists. Free marketeers. Supporters of entrepreneurism.

With heart. Lots of heart.

But at the end of the day, ***money is one of the spiritual forces of this universe*** — constructed by the force, enormity and insistence of the will of human beings over centuries. It is the way we provide safety, show love and enjoy the richness of the world.

(That's why we're thrilled to partner with people who want to convert what they love – their talents and their gifts – into real-world value, value that others want to be a part of).

It wasn't that long ago you could put a crappy, uninspired product out and wrap it up with some zippy marketing and make a cool couple of million. Threads of this still exist today. Just look at pop country music.

But that's not you. You want to do it right. You want to maintain your integrity.

The first thing you need to do is to accept you have genuine talents that can create value for other people in the world. Without this acceptance, you can't become a brand. At best, you can become a moderately well-marketed entity.

The second thing to embrace is that your particular set of gifts, passions and talents is perfectly designed for some audience out there. But if you don't get behind these gifts and express them, you're just singing in the shower.

There's a beautiful moment in our work of intrinsic branding when our clients awaken to a truth: that their gift is their mission and their business. They are all interconnected in order to make a dent in the universe.

The third idea to roll around between your ears is that you need to get specific. Like, really specific. We have observed for many people, the phrase, "we help people get better" is what they believe their brand promise to be. While we know there is a lot more underlying this truth than that and uncovering the deeper truth at the heart of intrinsic branding, this is not specific enough.

You have to know how to name and describe your talent — without run-on sentences and marketing speak. This needs to be sans copious explaining. It needs to be a direct, tangible expression, both of your abilities and of the directly related value to your audience.

We're going to be blunt here. This last exercise is likely not something you can do alone. The chances of you being successful at crafting this language are about one in a million. Outside of Lloyd Christmas, nobody thinks those are very good odds. You need an editor, a truth-teller and a bullshit detector.

In most cases, the value you think you bring is not the value in the mind of your audience.

The real value is usually hidden in some other ability you have, which you are currently taking for granted or overlooking because you think others might not care.

Uncovering this is also where you are going to need assistance from someone who knows you, understands the dynamics of modern business and has mapped portions of the human soul. If you are not in a position to engage with someone to help you uncover this truth, we suggest you pair up with a partner, an extremely close friend or even a child (they have a wonderful ability to spot the truest thing we say) to share some of your deep work with. They can act as a tuning fork for what you have excavated from your soul.

What happens if you don't do this? Nothing.

Ultimately, all of this is up to you. Doing nothing or doing something. Your choice.

But Wayne Dyer said it quite nicely: **"Don't die with the music still in you."**

Your talent is your music. It is not in you to be hoarded or doubted. It is meant to be sung.

Maybe occasionally a little too loud and a little off key, but that's OK.

It's the music that produces the value. Because it can be bought, consumed, shared and experienced, which is the very essence of creating a real, true brand.

HOW DO WE CREATE A MARKET POSITION?

Like "authenticity," "story" and the term "branding" itself, the concept of having a "market position" is one that causes business folks to lick their lips and lean in precipitously.

Most brands attempt some variation of a positioning statement, albeit lackluster or inaccurate. The concept of market position was introduced way back in 1981 by Al Ries and Jack Trout in their book, *"Positioning: The Battle for Your Mind."*

The Ries-Trout positioning formula has held up well, but does requires some updating to modern realities. Our favorite update on this topic comes from *"Play Bigger: How Rebels and Innovators Create New Categories and Dominate Markets"* by Al Ramadan, Christopher Lochhead, Dave Peterson, and Kevin Maney.

What's most glaringly different in the 21st century is how we go about gaining attention, addressing audience fragmentation and competing in the face of product-saturation. In other words, there's more noise, more distraction, more competition than ever in today's market. And none of these conditions will end any time soon.

Yet, everyone wants a strong, well-defined set of position differentiators that make them stand out in the marketplace.

Kind of like abs.

(And given the commoditization of marketing over the last decade, there's this prevailing mentality that things like market position can be "got." As if your director of marketing can just purchase a market position like she can buy a new CRM).

Few players actually know what market position truly is — and how to effectively articulate it.

Modern positioning is clearly establishing the reason why anyone should give you their precious attention and money.

Contemporary positioning is three-part alchemy:

1. **Understanding and articulating the unspoken need of the audience.** Traditional positioning does delve into the needs of the marketplace. In the pre-digital age, this made positioning a direct line of sight between your offering and, then, your audience. But as Steve Jobs once famously said, "… people don't know what they want until you show it to them." You must dig deeper into the soul of the audience — into the human beings who comprise the audience. You must listen beneath the surface language.

If you're assigning this piece to an exploration of "the pain," you are missing opportunities to know so much more about the humans who purchase from you —

what they hope for, what they fear, what they desire. (In our work with clients, they are frequently delighted to find their intuition was right all along. Their gut knew more about this unspoken need than their mind did).

2. **Heralding the courage and resources to create a new category if you can't be #1 or #2 in an existing one.** To understand contemporary category design, you must first embrace this: there is no #3 in the market. There are just a whole bunch of brands that are not #1 or #2.

Category creation is not for the timid because it requires you to go into uncharted waters outside of the comforting solid ground of ad campaigns, competitive analysis and focus groups. It requires you to push back against your peers who fear change. It requires you to spend resources educating the market on this new category. But the payoff is enormous if you have the fortitude. In short, be the most consistently excellent player in this category, and you will win.

3. **Offering products that are easy to talk about, easy to buy, and easy to use.** No amount of marketing language and ad copy, no tagline, can make up for poor quality, bad customer experience and inconsistent support. This is why the foundation of the brand, which when put into practice, results in superior positioning, must be determined as early in the launch process as possible. Old positioning was about being top of mind while the human experience was far less of a factor.

Modern positioning is about becoming the word-of-mouth king or queen.

It's no longer possible to have a solid market position without a solid brand. So, we'd caution you not to fall into the trap of thinking you can buy market position — or a brand.

That idea is a relic of the ad age.

A market position is a result of knowing who you are as a brand and what value you provide to the people who invest in your offerings and then telling that story consistently over time.

P.S. By rating yourself and your company on how consistently you practice the three aspects mentioned above indicate how well you are currently doing in creating and holding a unique market position.

WHAT DOES CULTURE HAVE TO DO WITH BRAND?

We are a handful of years into the Human Age.

In the 21st century, leaders must go beyond taking care *of* their people to embodying a new level of caring *for* people.

Taking care of your people is a minimum requirement – compensation, benefits, work environment. And even in the Human Age economy, there are still plenty of places to work that are sweatshops and boiler rooms – just with healthy food, beer taps and ping pong tables.

Caring for your people is seeing that each human on your team contains enormous value – not just for the work they do for you, but because of the substance of their souls. Contained within each of them is the power to grow your brand … or not.

The clients we work with understand this, at some level. They are working, in their own ways, and at their own pace, to embrace this idea. But it's hard.

It's fun to embrace this idea when you are thinking about how you as the leader can help your favorite team members become better leaders.

It's difficult and challenging when you consider nixing the leadership retreat/golf outing to host a surprise leadership-in-service day at a local soup kitchen. Or abandon your anti-Human Age policy of working a year before giving your people a week off or blocking all social media access.

These are tougher assignments.

In the 21st century we must *move the people* to move the numbers — as opposed to the 20th-century thinking that had that reversed.

That means loving the people.

Loving **them**.

Sharing the love with them.

Some people have asked us what culture has to do with branding.

The humans who make up your brand *are your brand*.

How they treat the work they do for your brand is a direct reflection of how you treat them. It's also a reflection of how you treat yourself as the leader, and then a reflection of how you treat the people around you. Conglomerated, this becomes how you choose to lead the organization — ie, sustainably or with a rode-hard-and-put-away-wet ethic.

What this means for you — the leader — is that your first investment in your culture needs to be in you.

It needs to be in uncovering how you are motivated, and why you are motivated to do this work.

Your people are dying to hear it from you! This is a key element of their motivation — not just the number of zeros on their paycheck.

Our intrinsic branding practice always begins with an examination of current conditions and an intense focus on the beliefs that underlie you.

As we enter the Human Age, talk is cheap — and boring.

Action is expensive — meaning it will cost you, as the leader, something personal and spiritual to take a stand against what were once acceptable leadership practices in the 20th century. But action is also riveting to your audience.

Simon Sinek said it best — people don't really buy what you are selling. They buy the feeling they get when they work with your brand.

So, what motivates your customers to buy from you? The same thing that motivates people to work for you: love and trust. When you tap into the humanity of your audience, you are making a deposit of trust. You are reminding them they're appreciated, valued and important.

You are making them part of your culture.

What robs a company culture or customer base of love and trust? Hypocrisy, inconsistency and manipulative tactics – just to name a few.

One of the things we rail against is the pervasive the-ends-justify-the-means way of doing business. That it is OK to manipulate people. That it is OK to dehumanize people for your financial benefit (this extends to your people and to your audience). We say hell no to that.

This is why we have a warning label on our website. Why we walk away from deals that require a compromise of our value and values. We don't do this just to be rebellious. We do it because we want to live out what we expect of the leaders we coach.

Ideas and principles are made real by behavior. So, what are you going to DO differently or better in the Human Age?

What sort of Human Age leader will you be?

WHAT IS YOUR BRAND'S MLE (MINIMUM LEVEL OF EXCELLENCE)?

A brand is an organic, living thing. It is both a practice and a discipline.

And yet there is also a baseline, or minimum, level of organic environmental excellence to create for your brand to grow and thrive.

Without this brand primordial soup, you may inadvertently stunt the growth of your brand and reduce its vibrancy and reach.

Most people begin working on their brand by focusing on the most external element. The first question we typically get around branding is: By branding, you mean logo, right?
Not quite. Yes, you need a level of visual appeal and digital presence. But those are baseline requirements for any organization.

To reach a level of excellence as a brand, leaders need to look within first. As achievers, leaders are well served to go on the inward journey required to create clarity and uncover their core beliefs — both personally and professionally. Yes, both are relevant, and both matter immensely in regard to what they are building.

This inward journey may seem counterintuitive in a business environment relentlessly obsessed with the external output. But it actually creates a sustainable, rich and healthy foundation all other cultural health, business development, and brand growth will rise from.

That's why our first branding MLE is to articulate your core beliefs and standards. Once you have cultivated and understood the soil of soul in which you are growing, which we help clients do during a Root Session, it's time to take a slightly larger look at the environment around you.

The world is a tidal wave pulverizing you with demands for your attention, action, and prioritization. It is a crushing environment for all humans armed with ancient brains slowly evolving to filter out much of the noise and somehow find harmony for our lives. In this space, most of the demands, requests, and shouts present in similar shrill tones, menacing memes, and dark, descriptive language.

A business and its leaders must not only be different but also must understand, with microscopically clear emotional intelligence, why their experience is different. Once you understand that, and have named it, the task is to share that differentiation, consistently and clearly, in the marketplace.

That's why the second branding MLE is to create obvious differentiation in the marketplace.

To create a MLE with differentiation requires leaders to go beyond standard campaign pablum to strategically and intentionally owning a conversation in the marketplace. This takes courage and insight. It takes a willingness to be bold. And it means honestly answering the question, "What makes us truly different?" For a starting point of differentiation look at the human factors. Your culture, your customer experience, your social voice. The humans in and around your brand are way more interesting than your offerings.

Differentiation will inform what you share with the market, with your ideal audience, but it is far from the most important content you create.

Since the beginning of time, humans have gathered to hear and be swept away by stories. Stories are always engaging to us. They are ways we come open-hearted and open-minded to learn without realizing that's what we are doing. They are how we understand the soulful underpinnings of another person's perspective, of an organization's true and real organizing principles. They are where trust begins.

As a modern brand, you must share your message and story in a way that invites and inspires, which is the third MLE. Avoid the Old World approach to story, one centered around igniting fear, uncertainty and doubt, catastrophe and chaos, leading to manipulation and coercion. Focus instead on stories of failing and overcoming, desperation and hope, tales featuring everyday heroes, novel ideas with merit.

Share stories that illustrate your unique set of beliefs and standards and how they are lived out. Tell the world why you are here, why you are doing this and what mountain you are headed out to climb.

Tell these stories in a modern way: in an engaging narrative, in visuals, in video retelling. Imagine sitting around a fire to share a little bit about what you do — where would you begin the story of your business if you were presenting your story that way?

A client of ours, Stream Logistics, a concierge logistics company that has three times been named to the Inc 500|5000 list of fastest growing companies, practices all three of these MLEs on a regular basis. They first did the work to articulate the beliefs in a Root Session, and they now share their standards in artful renderings on the walls of their office, in their hiring practices, in daily recognition, and in meetings. They tell stories during staff meetings of how they are embodying those standards. In daily sales conversations, they share with their audience the key differences they bring to all they do, emphasizing what it means to be a concierge logistics provider in an industry that has neglected accountability and personal service for years.

Another client, Terri Broussard Williams, is growing a movement maker tribe. She has begun her work toward turning moments into movements by sharing her story and the stories of other women who are making change happen in the world. She embodies her beliefs in the work she takes on, in the volunteer work she invests herself fully into and in the beautiful and inspiring content and products she is creating.

Finally, our client Intend2Lead organized their entire brand, business model and coaching practice around the mission and message uncovered in their Root Session. In a space (accounting) full of institutional thinking and sameness, they boldly use words like "love" and "truth." In essence, their entire brand presence is a mirror of their own character, excellence and value.

Wherever you are with your brand, take a breath. Be there. You may accept you have a couple MLEs firmly in place. You may acknowledge there is work to do on others.

Above all, avoid getting lost in the tidal wave of demands and their lure to focus instead on tactics that are perhaps easier to discuss, to sell and to do.

True navigation and true excellence come when you can identify true north.

HOW MUCH MONEY SHOULD I SPEND ON ADVERTISING?

As little as possible, mate.

Surprised?

You've been taught to believe that advertising is a necessity.

You've been trained to think that when you invest in marketing, you must buy ads or purchase some failsafe tactic or system. You've also been trained that marketing and advertising are synonymous and that marketing overall is a cost center.

No and no and no.

Marketing becomes a revenue center when it is executed as an artful and soulful expression of your brand.

The best brands understand this. See …

Yeti.

Spiritual Gangster.

IKEA.

Target.

Subaru.

Sure, these brands spend money on marketing – but not just on box-checking, budget-spending activities. Every marketing activity is centered around promoting the idea and feeling behind the brand.

Here are five things to spend your precious marketing dollars on:

1.   **Develop the leadership skills of your marketing team members.** To move the numbers, you must move the people. That includes your marketing numbers. Do not relegate your marketing leader to the position of order taker. If you instead elevate her or him — as a human, as a professional, as a strategic thinker — you will gain additional business savvy on your executive team and results in the marketing realm. How to do this? Encourage them to work with a brand coach, attend professional events or join a mastermind group.

2.   **Build a community.** We are firmly convinced that once you have the foundational elements of brand nailed down (mission, message, category, visuals, digital, content — all work that is done during the process of intrinsic branding), your best money is spent on building community. The first community is the one within your walls – your employees. Then your customers. Shower them with attention. Make them famous. Elevate employees and customers to be the face of your brand — not just your executives.

3.   **Content. Content. Content.** Today, every brand worth their salt is an inspiration or information source. If you do not view your public presence as an

opportunity to educate your audience, you are missing out. This doesn't mean cutting-and-pasting from your industry website or purchasing canned content. It means allocating resources to tell stories. Think like a small-town newspaper.

4.   **Experiences**. This covers a large swathe but definitely includes digital experiences (web, social, online events) and live experiences such as in-person events. Experiences are conversation generators. They get people talking to each other about your brand in ways that advertising and PR simply can't beat.

5.   **Activities that stimulate or accelerate word-of-mouth.** Word-of-mouth is not generated by bathing yourself in bold, meaningless and completely subjective platitudes such as, "We are the industry leader." To generate word-of-mouth, you must first make people *feel* what you stand for. You must speak in simple, unexpected and emotional ways about your mission, your message and invite people to share them in some real way (see experiences). The more real and delightfully surprising the activity you can present, the better.

What to not spend marketing dollars on?

Demographic-based campaigns. Demographics are only sometimes useful data sets; relics of the "Mad Men" age where large groups had predictable buying and media consumption habits.

Complicated marketing technology. This includes complex CRM systems, social media management and web platforms. Large brands can absorb the financial and energy suck of complexity but the rest of us have plenty of access to inexpensive, agile technology.

Lists. For the most part, the best part of purchasing a list is the opportunity to become a spammer. Yes, that's the best part. Here's a simple rule: have you ever bought anything from being emailed by a random stranger?

To directly answer the "how much money should I spend on marketing?" question, we posit this. The most valuable asset you have in your brand are the people who touch brand — employees and customers. So, invest in them with this simple formula: allocate $100/year per each human who touches your brand.

If you invest in the "yes" list and say hell no to the "no" list, you will be 80 percent ahead of most brands.

But to make you even more successful in your marketing endeavors, consider doing a deep dive into the meaning of your brand. The roots, if you will. As a good friend of ours was describing to us recently, "The people at this company are good people, but they've been doing what they do for years and years and years and they have forgotten completely why."

We'd love to help you remember.

HOW DO I SHARE MY MESSAGE WITH THE WORLD?

We often work with clients who have discovered the work that's behind them is not the work that's in front of them.

They've discovered it's not their life's work.

It's not what lies at the center of their heart.

It is not the impact they want to make.

Maybe you have found your way to this point as well. And now you've decided the time has come to redress the balance and spend your resources on realizing a new direction. It took a lot of work to get here. Welcome.

It's a good place to be. Also it's a half-terrifying, half-thrilling, overwhelming place to be.

So, where do you begin? Here are four initial ideas to wrestle with:

1. **Realize your new rulebook is drastically different than the one that got you here.** Sneak peek into the new rules: You don't need to work a 40-plus hour week or earn a six-figure salary tomorrow to prove your value. You don't need to fill your calendar

with meaningless meetings. You can do less and actually get more. Self-care will become a daily habit. Being a well-rounded person will be more indicative of your success than the hours you put in. Adaptability will be your best friend. There will be no one strategy that will work. A flexible mindset and diverse approach will be more lucrative. Repeated failure (also known as lessons or early efforts at success) is the new success.

2.   Realize the worlds of marketing, communication and branding have drastically changed and to be successful, you're going to have to opt-in to it. There's not much room, time or tolerance to cast a dismissive or suspicious eye on the tools of new marketing — social media conversations, consistent original content, spiritual connection with a defined audience. You must engage – now – and leave the comfort of the old world behind. Here's the upside: What you share, post, create or write will continue to work for you even after you've forgotten all about it.

3.   Re-examine your relationships. No one accomplishes anything alone. Especially not something incredibly difficult to achieve, a bit nebulous and counter to what most people do. You are going to need to understand how your dearest relationships will – or won't support you on your quest to become this next evolution of you. Some may fall away – some may sing your praises and fill your emotional sails on bad days. Either of these are preferable to those near to you who want to stick around and criticize, undermine or stifle your endeavor. Their intentions aside, the last thing you need are uninformed opinions. The best method here: have a deeply honest conversation about where you are heading and who you need surrounding you. Then let the relationship cards fall where they might.

4.   Get clear on your message. This is one of your very first steps as a brand and as a business. That's why it is the heart of what we uncover during our intrinsic branding work. Without a message, you have nothing to say. And word-of-mouth is still the most effective way to attract people to you. It is the root of your story, the carrier of your ideas and an invitation to believe what you believe. It can't be good enough. It has to be rock solid and feel like the most important thing you say all day. Your message is a bridge to the real you. It's the first way people will experience what you are becoming and where you are going.

These are heady moments and you should enjoy them. But there will be moments when you ask, "What have I done!?"

We would say, "Keep going!"

Fear is a fog you must pass through to reach your destination. It's not a reason to stop.

The biggest pitfall to avoid is the idea that you are alone in this. You're not.

We're here.

HOW TO TURN BRAND ANXIETY INTO BRAND INTELLIGENCE

You've been going along and growing your company. You are a good leader, and you have a good heart. And you are good at what you do. You have confidence in your competence as a business person.

But there's this itchy sensation that comes over you whenever you consider the way you are marketing your company. Very simply stated: it is not quite right yet.

Nagged by one sense that something is off, you've tried and failed to attack the issue, but truth be told: you don't have much more insight to add, which only increases your sense of unease.

Yet, you can't forget it. You can't let it go. Your instinct is telling you this issue lies at the very heart of your business. As a leader who has gotten this far, you know in perfect clarity that your instincts are very important — and usually right on.

Here's our take: This frustrating feeling — one that keeps telling you something is off.

It's a good thing. It's presenting you with an opportunity to address a weakness.

The weakness you feel, you sense, is that your brand has not been articulated, has not been explained and has not truly been captured.

It's very natural to gravitate toward taking action in areas you feel most competent. Primarily because we humans don't like those feelings of inadequacy, so we work on what we know. And most entrepreneurs don't really know branding. Increasing branding confidence is one of the areas we focus on with leaders and their organizations. We refer to this as brand intelligence.

Brand intelligence is awareness of and active engagement in the creation of your mission-based brand — integrating art, language, culture and experience.

Brand intelligence can only be increased with daily practice and making that practice a core competency for you and everyone on your team.

So we posit this: the key to ridding yourself of those uneasy feelings is to raise your brand intelligence.

Here are some fundamentals to explore:

Admit you don't know. Entrepreneurs create blindspots by thinking they know. Once you admit you don't know something, say for instance, when you admit you don't know much about branding, then and only then can you truly learn about it.

Consciously and deliberately consider that your (personal) mission has a direct line of sight into your business. It is informing your business, daily, and it has been since you began. Do not panic if you don't know what your personal mission is yet. We will help you uncover what you already know it to be deep inside.

Once you begin to warm to this idea, begin to shift your thinking to making your mission the center of your brand, not your business model. When your business model is at the center of your brand, there's a tendency to let branding become a linear, short-term afterthought. You simply can't raise your brand intelligence if you aren't focusing on brand at a strategic level.

Consider that brand is how other people experience what you believe. If you are part of the founding team, you will forever and always have the unofficial role of chief spiritual officer. You are responsible for not just the wellbeing of your team, but the spiritual essence and belief system of your culture. This is not HR's job to handle.

As a leader, if you are feeling anxious about how your business is showing up in the world, take a deep breath before you push that feeling away. Humans have been conditioned to believe that anxiety automatically means something is wrong. We see it differently, especially for entrepreneurs.

Anxiety is there to tell us something important has come onto our radar that needs your special attention. As the chief spiritual officer, you are equipped to handle it, despite what your brain is telling you.

By not ignoring it, you give your brand a chance to truly come to life. And that means progress, opportunity for growth, and a chance to be excellent.

And we know you like that.

5 SIMPLE WAYS TO IMPROVE YOUR BRAND IN ONE DAY

We both love mornings. They bring with them the promise of the day, the hope of a new habit or opportunity. And great coffee.

So, if today is the day you set aside to immediately improve your brand, what are you going to do? Drawing a blank? Have no fear, here are five things you can do right now.

1. **Share from the soul.** If you are already engaging on social media, stop talking about things you really do not care about. Stop sharing for the sake of sharing. Give yourself a day away from shares, RTs or reposts. Come up with one idea that makes you feel something, then share that. Give yourself permission to share an idea that frightens you a bit – or feels vulnerable. In a world of social pretense and CGI-ed polish, being raw and real is a huge brand advantage.

2. **Burn your dress code.** Let your employees wear what they want and speak according to their personality.

This will quickly inject a burst of originality into your culture. It's normal to feel fear in the face of this advice, but people who feel they are able to express themselves at work are much more likely to be engaged in the work they do. This goes for you too. Remember this: "business casual" is typically just code for "be safely boring."

3. **Infuse some art.** If you are a human who enjoys drawing pictures or have been accused of doodling during meetings, stop and pay attention to your art. Then think about the ways you could add this art or art inspired by it, to your brand. What do we mean? Could there be a hand-drawn element posted to your website, to explain a service or product? Could all of these doodles become a one-time or series of blog posts? Could that little doodle evolve into a powerful graphic that explains your philosophy of beliefs as an organization?

4. **Start a new conversation.** Send a "conversation starter" out to your customers that can be converted to content. Example: ask them what is one thing they are working on that will change the world? Then ask how you can support them in their efforts. This will spark a bunch of conversations, provide acres of content and help remind your customers that you are their partner in whatever movement they are starting.

5. **Ask a simple question.** Ask your employees one simple question. Rather than extensive employee surveys, one simple question can stir change, remind

your employees of their value and reinforce that you are a 21st century leader. For example, ask them this question: What is one thing you would change if you were the CEO (or owner)? Then listen to the responses. Set aside time to read through them and ponder them without judgement or response from you. After a good amount of musing time takes place, thank them for their responses and work to select one or two you can implement or openly discuss.

Becoming a modern brand has a thousand moving parts. It is a mysterious blend of practical habits, savvy strategy and unexplainable magic. It can be crazy overwhelming. It can feel impossible. But hopefully, these five acts show you how simple activities can immediately impact your brand and remind you how much control you have over your brand – and that some actions simply require leadership.

TOP 10 SIGNS YOUR BRAND IS OPTING IN TO THE 21ST CENTURY

Do you find yourself grappling with how to take the 20th century equity in your business and brand and remain relevant in the modern marketplace? You're not alone.

Most established leaders today find themselves at a yes/no moment. You can say yes and opt-in to become a 21st century brand. Or you can choose to opt-out – or the market will opt you out. We hope all leaders say yes and opt in! The world needs your experience, wisdom and insight.

You may already be on your way to opting in and becoming a 21st century brand. Consider these top 10 traits of 21st century brands to see how your brand is evolving:

1. You live for a purpose beyond just making money.
2. You have a consistent, authentic presence on at least one form of social media.
3. Your clients and/or employees love you, and they spread your message for you.
4. Your visual brand is polished and contemporary
5. Your message clearly articulates why you are different.

6. You've carefully created client experiences that inspire rave reviews.
7. Your employees love working for you and understand their connection to your mission.
8. You regularly write and share compelling content that intrigues people.
9. You are a trusted resource for the media.
10. Others consider you the gold standard in your industry.

Every leader is capable of achieving all 10 of these signs with the right intention and guidance — especially when they truly commit to opt-in.

RE-BRANDED? NOT UNLESS YOU'VE DONE THESE 5 THINGS

When people tell us they've been through a re-brand, first we get excited.

Then we get curious. Then we ask what the effort entailed.

"Oh, a new logo and tagline."

Then we get sad. Wah-wah.

We get sad because we care. Because to us, your brand is more than your visual representation, and it's more than a schmaltzy, cheesier description of your product or service.

Re-branding by creating some new visuals and a snazzy tagline is like going to the fair without riding the roller-coaster. You missed out!

So, what is a re-brand? What does it really entail?

1. Branding is first a spiritual experience, and so is a re-brand. A re-brand is first an **invigoration of your mission, values and vision**. This critical step is essential because companies tend to drift away from these moorings over time. By re-connecting to these

three essentials, you remind yourself, your leadership team, employees and customers of your purpose and value in the world.

2. A re-brand often requires a house-cleaning. **A purging of the old to make space for the new**. This can be literal (like an old website or marketing material) or more intangible (like old ideas and old thinking). This requires casting a skeptical eye on all parts of your brand and seeing what stays, what gets re-purposed and what needs to be hauled off to the local Goodwill.

3. When preparing to re-introduce your brand to the world, it's important to understand that everything should be up for review and consideration. This requires a **re-examination of your business model, product lines, and pricing strategy**. A re-branding can't just be new packaging of the same ol', same ol'. That just creates cynicism with employees and yawning from customers.

4. When facilitated correctly, a re-brand will **naturally create innovation in your organization**. A re-brand should always entail bringing relevant stakeholders to the discussion party and hearing from them about the places the brand promise is strong and the places where it is worn. In a healthy organization, this leads to discussion about how you can improve that worn-out experience with innovative ideas and efforts. It should also generate the energy for people to tackle these

initiatives. If your re-brand didn't do that, it's a sign it might not have been an inclusive-enough effort.

6. It is an absolute must to **invite your employees, customers and influencers** to actively participate in the re-brand. This is why announcing a new logo or new website as a "re-brand" is often met with apathy. The people who touch your brand own your brand. They share their feelings and ideas outside of the traditional constraints of business. When enrolled, they take this enthusiasm into their circles of influence as an expression of themselves.

It's important to set your expectations of the timeline and impact of a re-brand. A re-brand is not a one-time event. It's not a big splash and then a fading-back-to-average. Plan on at least a six-month roll-out – with a series of events organized around your various audiences, refreshed content and – if called for – a new logo and website.

And if asked about the ROI on a re-brand, we have this handy reply for you to use: **"What's the ROI of having a brand everyone in this organization loves?"**

SECTION 2:
Leading is Branding

ARE YOU A DEFIANTLY DRIVEN LEADER?

We often get the question, "Who do you work with?" Most times, the questioner expects us to list an industry, a company's size, a revenue level.

Nope.

We say, "We work with defiantly driven leaders who want their brand to be a monument to what they believe."

So, what does that truly mean?

As it turns out, defiantly driven leaders possess three core traits, which manifest in a number of powerful ways in the business world.

We determined the three core traits of defiantly driven leaders are:

High EQ (Emotional Intelligence/Quotient) – Defiantly driven leaders have a great awareness of self, others, situations, strategy and unplanned leadership moments. That means they understand their relationships deeply, their strengths and weaknesses, and the emotional dynamics of others. In tense or emotional situations, they are able to remain self-possessed and clear about who they are and what the best action to take is.

Heart for Others – Defiantly driven leaders genuinely care about other people and also practice self-care. They espouse servant leadership, where they look to serve others before themselves. They are listeners, reflectors and want to lead after they have carefully considered how their actions will impact others in their organization and the world. They recognize when they are run down, fearful or in an uncertain place and are able to step back to recalibrate themselves. They are in tune with their heart when making direction-changing decisions.

Mission-centric – Defiantly driven leaders have souls on fire with a purpose. They view their business is an extension or fulfillment of their personal mission. All business decisions run through the filter of "Does this align with our/my mission?" They trust both kinds of data – hard data and intuition.

That all sounds nice, right? But how does being a defiantly driven leader manifest in the business world? The ROI of being awake and driven is a continuum of both short- and long-term value creation, but here are a few benefits.

- A defiantly driven leader's high standards of excellence about, well, everything, increase the overall productivity and performance of a business. These high standards remove the myth of perfection and replace it with habits of excellence. High standards give guidance to the "yeses" and "no's" leaders have to make every day. The financial benefit is higher output and improved quality.

- A defiantly driven leader is essentially the "chief spiritual officer —" meaning they are the one person in the organization who holds the meaning, beliefs and values above all else. This creates a brand with a soul, which in turn creates a natural attractant for both talent and customers. The financial benefit is that recruiting, and customer acquisition costs are much lower.

- Defiantly driven leaders have a willingness to invest — in their people, in the right systems, and in building a brand rich with meaning. They are discerning about their investments, but see the value in developing depth of humans, depth of efficiency and depth of meaning. The financial benefit is loyalty of their people, greater talent inside the building, steady growth and stable profitability.

- This may be the most immediately recognizable outcome of being a defiantly driven leader: customer experiences that create delight. Delight is such a rare experience for grown-ups. But these leaders have a child-like wonderment and joy for seeing other people enjoy unexpected happiness. Therefore, they want to create that experience again and again in their business dealings. When they — and their teams — do so, the financial benefit is enormous: starting with much lower advertising costs, reduced headcount for customer maintenance, and streamlined operating costs.

If these traits or benefits resonate with you, it's likely you are a defiantly driven leader. That doesn't necessarily mean you work at the top of your organization, or have a group of people working under you. Defiantly driven leaders are found in every part of every organization and in every size of business.

Don't let anyone tell you that being the sort of leader you are is "squishy" or that it doesn't benefit the business. Frankly, that's bull honky. Being defiant and driven is the greatest business advantage of the 21st century.

HOW BEING A SOULFUL LEADER BOOSTS YOUR BRAND

There are a lot of business people who balk at the use of the term "soul." They think it has no place in the professional world.

We think differently (but you knew that already).

To us, the most powerful type of leader is a leader who is soulful in a variety of ways — they deeply understand who they are, they are intensely aware of why their company exists, and they are fully engaged in the well-being of their first customers — their employees. We have embraced the term "spiritual intelligence" to describe these leaders: intuitive, insightful, introspective and having high initiative. They love themselves, they love people and it shows in their brands.

They are not executive box checkers. They believe and embrace the true role of a soulful leader — acting as the CSO, chief spiritual officer, of the brand. A few examples of soulful leaders to illustrate our point: Oprah, Brene Brown, Ellen DeGeneres, LeBron James, and Richard Branson.

Being a soulful leader is not something you reach after you meet your numbers. It's not the same as being a kind person at work. Being a soulful leader is a tremendous competitive advantage over traditional leaders who put all of their belief into the math and none into the magic.

While the idea of soul in business is rising, there's still plenty of leaders who need to stop hitting the snooze button on finding their soul and applying it to business. To give you a little motivation to look inward, here are five ways being a soulful leader boosts your brand. If you're one of these soulful bosses, enjoy and put these to work. If not, well, read on…

1. **By communicating with message clarity.** Traditional leaders hire ad agencies to tell them what their message should be in order to reach a target market. Soulful leaders speak from their hearts and this produces an endless supply of ideas, concepts and offerings. Example: Southwest Airlines speaks openly about their "soul," and their promotions are always anchored to this idea. Soulful leaders are the lead evangelist for their brand and don't need publicists, preppers or polishers to talk about why and what they believe. They live and breathe the message.

2. **By accessing the power of organic consistency.** The old model of command-and-control was designed to create efficiency and productivity. However, in the new world, this approach stifles culture and slows communication. Soulful leaders have created daily habits of innovation, empathy and value creation. This organic approach makes their organizations much more agile and functionally consistent. It allows them to fail quickly on ideas that don't work and rapidly scale the ones that do. It also harnesses the power of their

employees and customers as living quality assurance and research & development teams.

3. **By preventing an identity crisis.** Brands carry the same traits as the people who lead them. Many established brands are dealing with an identity crisis because the individual leaders are too. The whole world has changed, and they are frozen in place – not knowing who they are and how they fit in. Soulful leaders have never really had a brand identity crisis. They understand that trends come and go, so they rarely derive their value from them. Unlike their traditional counterparts, they see change as a positive – as an opportunity to evolve, grow and compete. They don't need to have people tell them who they are – they just need to remember to return to the root of their soul.

4. **By branding beyond a department.** In top-down organizations, branding is an activity or an initiative — or maybe a strategy. To these leaders, branding has a beginning, middle and end. This thinking creates compartmentalized, check-box thinking that relegates the soul of a brand to spreadsheets and committees. But in reality, the branding effort is never done. Brands led by soulful leaders understand this and make branding a daily habit of everyone in the organization. They understand their personal calling is their brand, and that this brand is reflected in the culture and the customer experience. They understand they are stewards of the brand and view employees, customers and communities as the true brand "owners."

5. **By closing the talent gap.** "Human capital" or "human assets" are the terminologies of soulless leaders who don't see people as individuals. Further, traditional hiring models create a blindspot based on technical skill and/or the ego-driven idea that your gut is your best indicator of a good hire. Neither is true in the modern world. Soulful leaders attract believers. When someone is on fire for what they believe in and what they believe in is why their company exists, the discussion around talent attraction becomes a lot simpler. Sharing the beliefs of the organization acts as an attractant to those who believe what you believe. Talented professionals today want to work in organizations that have high cultural EQ — leaders who know their feelings and can express them, particularly related to why their work matters.

Keep this in mind: the role of chief spiritual officer does not have to be an executive. It could be you. If you have a passion for your company's mission, if you are the voice of hope, if you are a spokesperson for the unheard, this role might be your calling. The key is to use these five ways, along with your own wisdom, to build momentum in your organization.

If you are the owner/CEO and you are a soulful leader, you can be certain the advantages of command-and-control leadership have had their day. A new day is dawning in business and other leaders need your help to let go of old notions and embrace the truth of why they matter in this new world.

AGELESS LEADERSHIP: OPTING IN TO THE NEW ERA

Today's leaders have become much more adept at recognizing the value of the millennial generation and at adopting new habits to incorporate them into business. But now, these leaders have another decision to make. Do they opt-in to the new business landscape created by 40 million tech-native millennials? Or do they just cautiously endorse from the sidelines?

So, what does "opt in" mean? And what is it going to cost these leaders to do it?

With five age groups in the workforce, there is a natural blending of ideas, cultures and habits taking place. This blending is producing opt-in leaders who have some common traits that transcend traditional labels related to age, ethnicity and gender. These opt-in leaders represent a new type of meritocracy as they recognize the unique value each generation brings in novel ways.

Leaders need to worry less about the associated cost and the changes being implemented by this generation and focus instead on how to personally opt-in in a complete and authentic way.

The first step to becoming an opt-in leader is understanding millennials don't view themselves as different. Most actually resent being labeled as a generation and view the changes they are bringing as reasonable and inevitable and a return to common sense. As such they are not opting in. They are already "in." And now they are becoming executives, business owners and community leaders.

Second, while some leaders are just more comfortable opting out, those who choose to opt-in are reaping the benefits of reinvigorated passion for leadership and life, the opportunity to give and receive mentoring and the chance to enjoy business prosperity accessed by new thinking.

Are you ready to opt-in? Here's what it looks like!

1. **Self-Awareness (EQ)** – This is reconnecting with yourself. The old leader is full of wisdom and experiences but was raised in an era when the changes millennials have brought about were the stuff of fiction. Therefore, the old leader dwells in fear, incredulity and doubt about the new world order. The opt-in leader is immersed in self-worth and appreciation of life experiences and a recognition of the intrinsic value of people — not things. They embrace change. The evidence of this rise in self-awareness is the explosion in popularity in yoga, spiritual enlightenment and the removal of the stigma of self-help.

2. **Self-Direction (Sovereignty)** – The top-down command-and-control leadership style is the dinosaur

of the modern business age. We're all just waiting for that last meteor to hit. Instead, opt-in leaders are embracing self-direction for themselves and the people who they lead by recognizing the individuality of people. Self-direction thinking includes leadership modeling, investing in the whole person, and doing work that matches your passion and individual intention. Rather than select people by resume and experience only, Opt-in leaders use cultural and job fit tools to ensure they have talent that also embraces self-direction. In the workplace, self-direction is experienced with flexible, open workspaces, options for working remotely, and company-endorsed entrepreneurial side gigs. The evidence of the rise in sovereignty is seen in start-ups, as well as established brands like Google, Amazon and Tesla.

3. **Tech Adoption (Innovation)** – This no longer means accepting whatever phone or computer the IT guy gives you. When you opt-in, you view technology as your best tool for connection, innovation and productivity. Opt-in leaders recognize selecting the right tools is a timeless competitive advantage. They also recognize that technology adoption is the leading indicator of relevance. How you feel about technology is also readily apparent to most people you interact with. Opt-in leaders actively seek out new ideas, new uses, new features in order to stay ahead of the game. While they likely won't camp overnight to get the latest iPhone, they might send an intern to do it for them.

4. **Cultural Exposure (Travel)** – Mark Twain once said the only cure for narrow-mindedness is travel. Simply put, opt-in leaders get out of the office. They travel to expand their sphere of understanding and influence. They go to conferences to soak up new ideas. They travel abroad to glean from other cultures. They consume documentaries and read voraciously about new frontiers, ideas and the history of wanderlust. In the workplace, opt-in leaders have an appreciation for different. While background and education are still valuable, they view alternative paths as rich with potential for their work and worth.

5. **Access to Resources (Investing)** – Those who opt-in fear being stuck or stale, so they reinvest in endeavors that expand their boundaries, thinking and knowledge. They have a decidedly entrepreneurial view of capital – both in time and money. While financial investing is part of this, opt-in leaders are likely to have diverse pursuits beyond a traditional portfolio. These may include angel investments in start-ups, side consulting practices and/or speaking and writing opportunities. In the workplace, they invest in their people through leadership development programs, wellness, flex time and mentoring.

General Douglas MacArthur once said, "Old leaders never die. They just fade away." With all due respect to the general and his corncob pipe, we disagree! Today's leaders have worked too hard for too long to be unfairly relegated to irrelevance. But they also need the courage to own this moment, recognizing the people they lead and who love them are waiting for them to opt-in.

THE BRAND ADVANTAGE OF AWAKE LEADERS

The world these days is like a hibernating bear at the end of winter. It's getting a bit warmer out, but it's always easier to stay asleep.

So, it is in the world of leadership, too.

Leaders today have every reason to awaken: it's good for their brand, it's good for their business, it's good for the people they lead — and it's extremely needed in the world right now.

And yet, too few are rousing themselves into becoming an awake leader — an individual who is mission-driven, loves people and feels called to improve the world. Awake leaders have high emotional intelligence (EQ), tend to view change as opportunity and are disciplined about self-care.

The opposite of an awake leader is what we refer to as an institutional leader. We are not condemning or scorning these institutional leaders. They serve in necessary roles for continuation of organizations and entities. But they've made the choice to turn over and hit snooze on their brand, on many aspects of their business, and on the development of their people — for the time being.

One area of stark contrast between awake and institutional leaders is how they see brand and branding.

Institutional leaders see brand and branding as marginally necessary activities for supporting a business model or organizational structure. A large portion of what forms this worldview about brand and branding is their 20th century mindset about advertising and promotion. Because of this bias, brand is very much an external focus on perception and image – what we call the "candy wrapper" of the brand.

Institutional leaders have a linear and literal mindset about brand. They love tactics: campaigns, slogans, marketing jargon to name a few. In addition, they tend to untether business strategy and brand strategy. They typically see people through the lens of a role or label: employee, customer, shareholder, vendor. They tend to be defensive about public mistakes or failures.

Awake leaders see brand as an essential foundation for their life and business. They see brand as an extension of their personal and business mission and beliefs. They weave their purpose into everything they do — including their brand and their business. For the awake leader, everyone matters, and labels are unimportant. They are just as likely to have an engaging conversation with the least influential team member as they are with their board of directors. They see brand as circular, not linear. Everything connects to everything else and things like culture, customer experience and innovation are all components of a contemporary brand.

Besides not snoring, awake leaders have a number of significant competitive advantages over brands led by institutional leaders, including:

- Quicker reactions to market changes and opportunities
- Faster get-to-market times
- Better recruiting, which leads to a more talented team, more productivity, efficiency and engagement

· Less spend on advertising and promotion because they understand and embrace the power of delight and word-of-mouth

· Constant innovation with new products, business models and social good

For those who choose to awaken themselves and their brands, these advantages will enable them to stand out among their audience, and offer modern value in a rapidly changing world.

WHY EGO KILLS BRANDS

To be a leader you need a healthy ego. Leading with your ego will kill your brand.

Discuss.

Not sure what to discuss? We got you.

First off, we need an ego. It keeps us alive and moving. It looks out for us and spurs urgency. This is why the ego makes a great employee but a terrible boss.

Leaders who allow the ego to lead are making themselves highly vulnerable to destruction.

Not just the destruction of their own brand or reputation, but the destabilization and potential razing of their business as well. Unfortunately, the more successful (financially, at least) an ego-driven leader is, the less likely they are to change. And the less likely they are to realize their ego is leading.

Because leading with your ego works. And it does for a long time.

But it does not work forever. (Cases in point: Trump, Musk, Kalanick and probably a dozen or so people you know in real life.)

Here's what leading with your ego looks like:

- Being numbers (and data) obsessed as an antidote for insecurity
- Taking highly emotional or personal reactions and making them policies
- Objectifying people as either targets to persuade or tormentors to rage against
- Willful ignorance of one's own power and influence on the people around you
- A cult of personality in one's organization or team

Here's how all that kills your brand ...
- Repeatedly allowing tactics to drive strategy
- Cost-cutting in the culture and customer experience
- Obsession with the competition
- Managing your image instead of just not acting like an asshole
- Crisis management expenses are a line-item
- You get fired from your own company, sued and ostracized

Soul-based leadership looks very different from this. Soul-based leaders are still achievers; they still have a drive to win. Just not at the expense of their soul, culture and brand.

They have made the conscious choice to get clear on what their mission is in life. They understand what their soul's imperative is in this life. And they have chosen to allow this to be the true driver of whatever endeavor they find themselves in — business or personal or philanthropic.

Unlike those driven by ego, soul-based leaders are others-minded, not self-centered.

They have the humility to understand it is their team of people who will make their goals real, not just themselves.

They have an insatiable curiosity and healthy skepticism that compels them to do things differently; to defy conventional wisdom and formulas.

They are not afraid of failure. In fact, most soul-based leaders encourage failure.

Most of all, soul-based leaders see the world differently. They see people and profits. They see possibility and problems. They see the past and the future. They see strategy and tactics.

Here are 10 ways being a soul-based leader shows up in your brand.

1. Your brand is rooted in truth and love, which means branding and marketing activities are the amplification of what's real, not the reinforcement of a construct.

2. You have a consistent strategy. Tactical pursuits always serve the strategic imperatives. And tactics are flexible, never rigid.

3. You have a heart-based message that everyone who touches the brand believes in.

4. You care about the way things feel, look and are experienced. Customer experience and people are the last places you look for cost-cutting.

5. You create and own a category that didn't exist before.

6. You choose to pay for retention (talent and customers) instead of paying for attention (advertising).

7. You know improving yourself improves the business, and you encourage everyone you know to do the same.

8. You are unafraid to share your deep beliefs, standards and mission with everyone inside your doors and outside your doors.

9. Failures are acknowledged – and then used as opportunities to grow the business.

10. There is an intentional but natural regeneration of your culture and your brand.

So we have a challenge for you.

Where do you think you are? Are you an ego-based leader? Or a soul-based one? More specifically, give yourself an honest 1-10 (10 being highest) rating on the above 10 traits.

And if you know Trump, Musk or Kalanick, please send them this excerpt. That would be fun.

YOU DON'T WANT TO BE DIFFERENT

You say you want to be different. You say you want to stand out from the crowd. You say you want to be bold. You say you want to be noticed.

Sorry, but we don't believe you.

Like alleged country music singers talking about how "country" they are, talking about being different usually means you are rife with boring sameness. Or perhaps you are trying to be some slightly better version of sameness. Either way …

Here are some signs you are falling into the chasm between uniqueness and sameness:

- You think your message to the world is some variation of "I help people get better.
- You say your target audience is "everyone."
- You believe you don't have competition.
- You believe in creating happy mediums, slogans and taglines for your businesses' marketing.
- You think a new logo fixes a stale or negative reputation.

The truth is your impulse to be different is stymied by your real, true case of FUD — fear, uncertainty and doubt. We aren't saying you shouldn't feel these things — they are evidence of being human. We are saying if you really want to be different, you will find a way to push through them to the other side. In essence, you will break your addiction to sameness and safety and embrace what truly makes you different.

If you truly want to be different, start doing these three things:

Listen. Listening is evidence of security, of being grounded. This means the things you need to listen to are not your brain, the data or your best friend's boyfriend who is a marketing guru. The first thing you do need to listen to is your heart, your intuition. The second thing to listen to is your surroundings – what are the people who touch your brand saying? What are your competitors saying? What are the unmet needs in the marketplace? Simply reacting to these is not enough. You need to truly LISTEN to what they are saying. Stop saying, "I know, I know." Just stop. Let the ideas settle in. Force yourself to ask three follow-up questions before making a judgment. For example, ask, "What's missing?", "What would make this more valuable?" and "Do you want this?"

Take Risks. People who are truly different take risks. They push back against status quo, they challenge norms and they agitate assumptions. We have lost a trio of these risktakers recently: Muhammad Ali, Prince and David Bowie. Before they were game-changers, they were dubbed as threats. This might not be a role you are willing to accept right now. Be honest in examining your soul on this point. Are you at a place in your life that you are ready to espouse and advocate for something challenging or very new? Another soul-check is this: do you get a large portion of your value from the acceptance of others? We all need outside validation now and again, but to chase this means you are not ready to be different.

Say No. A basic but often overlooked rule of branding is this: if you narrow your focus, you broaden your appeal. This takes extraordinary discipline because an inflated ego sees opportunity to waylay your intentions in every distraction. It convinces you that by focusing, you are missing out on something. Like a greedy fisherman, it tries to catch all of the fish in the lake instead of just focusing on the first fish. As your brand grows, it also means saying "no" to anything that violates your standards – especially related to the kind of culture you are creating. At the most basic level, saying no allows your heart and mind to expand by rejecting that which does not serve you. It simultaneously strengthens your resolve to focus on your most vital purpose.

So here is a real-life test for you try:
Ask 10–15 people this question: what am I doing that is truly different?

If this question unleashes several powerful responses from your tribe, and you believe the time is right for you to take your coffee shop band to the main stage, we want to hear your music.

5 SIGNS YOUR BUSINESS IS HAVING A MIDLIFE CRISIS

Midlife crises are fairly easy to recognize in others, but they're often not so easy to recognize in yourself—and sometimes even more difficult to recognize when it comes to your company.

Business owners have always had to grapple with marketplace changes, but now as a seasoned business owner, you are facing a new wave of trends such as a mobile workforce, social engagement with customers, unexpected competition from startups with slick marketing, disruptive new models of business, and generational shifts in leaders, employees, and customers. In the midst of these struggles, you may find yourself trapped between what you used to be and where you want to go next.

As your customers and employees get younger, you might feel surprisingly older and have the creeping feeling that you are out of touch. You used to be a trendsetter—the first to tell your peers about a new idea. There was a time when being relevant was easy, but now the pace of change has quickened, and you worry you are too far behind to join the race. Rather than being the next Uber of your industry, you are simply trying figure out how to convert all of your 20th century experience to new realities.

This is a midlife moment for your business. While you may be experiencing this phenomenon in a variety of unique ways, here are five signs that your company is having a midlife moment:

1. Brand Fractures. There's a distinct fissure between the past and the future. There are some people in your organization who are fiercely holding onto the past and others who are furiously pushing forward with little awareness for the legacy of the company. This creates an internal lack of clarity, as well as confusion in the marketplace, because people are unsure what your brand stands for.

2. Technology Gap. You use Facebook to keep up with your kids, grandkids and college buddies, but you're uncertain about the right approach to using technology as a marketing tool for your business. These insecurities are amplified by the fact that others in your industry have moved on with digital and social strategies that seem to be working.

3. Unawareness. Have you ever mentioned your favorite band from the 70s to an employee only to have them reply, "Who?" That may be happening with your brand, too! New competition, new marketing methods and massive amounts of noise and distractions have caused your brand to fade from top of mind to "never heard of them." Leaders must set aside ego and accept that reengaging with new audiences is part of opting in.

4. Staleness. The logo, collateral and website you used to love are starting to feel like leftovers that have been sitting in the fridge too long—and they sometimes even induce smirks on the faces of new hires and prospects. You know you need a change, but you don't want to lose the brand recognition you've already built by starting all over.

5. Attraction. Your brand has moved from attractive to acceptable. You find that while you are still earning business, it's from the same people you have always done business with. And when you are up to bat with a new prospect, your gold standard for closing the deal no longer works—forcing you to explain your value.

It's time to change. If you're experiencing any, or all, of these symptoms, then it's time to initiate change. The great news is that the values, work ethic, drive, and experience that got you here will be the cornerstone to help you build the next level.

You do know who you are, and you do know what makes your company awesome, even though the marketplace may not anymore. The solution is to tell your story, and to give your customers the opportunity to connect with the humans behind your brand to see a new, more relevant side of who you are—and what your brand stands for—today.

A renewed focus on branding and marketing will do wonders to push you past this midlife moment—and back into the driver's seat. Maybe the driver's seat of a red convertible.

3 CORPORATE HABITS THAT WILL CRUSH ENTREPRENEURIAL SPIRIT

We heart entrepreneurial people. We heart them wherever they may be, and whenever they might find us.

Recently, we've seen an increasing number of what we term ATLs, or "about-to-launch," folks who have finally found the corporate structure too oppressive to their souls to abide any longer. As they prepare their escape, they reach out to us. We meet at the junction and help these ATLs plan their next, more meaningful dedication of intellect, effort and purpose — what we would simply call the launch of their brand.

In every case, it's an absolute pleasure to help them define their mission, craft their message and coach them to become a brand.

But we've also learned that corporate habits are hard to break. That the linear structures and rigid systems of corporate life can run counter to entrepreneurial progress — even for those seeking greater freedom and control in their work.

In the years to come, there will only be more of these ATLs finding their footing.

Entrepreneurism in America has been on a steady incline since 2010 since its precipitous drop following the economic crisis of 2008-09. In 2015, nearly 680,000 new businesses were started, according to the United States Department of Labor.

Like immersion into any culture, corporate culture shapes your thinking, conditions your responses and informs your behavior. In a corporate environment, getting along and getting things done is, by necessity, a group effort. Pile on top of this corporate politics, market pressure, shareholder value — and you learn how to bite your tongue, lessen your true self and "do what's best for the company."

If you find yourself in the good company of ATLs, we encourage you to take some time to consider how your corporate habits will either support or hinder your entrepreneurial endeavors.

We've observed three pesky behaviors deeply ingrained in our budding heroes, which tend to block brands and stall progress.

> **Using a map but not a compass.** Serial entrepreneur and thought-leader Srinivas Rao uses this metaphor in his book, "The Art of Being Unmistakable." He points out that corporate life is all about the map: knowing where you're going, planning a route and following a plan. In the entrepreneurial life, there is rarely a map, but there is a compass.
>
> In our language, this compass is your "Mission and your Root Belief." When you get lost (and you will!), your Mission and your Root Belief are your true north. When you need to make a decision, your compass will tell you which way to turn. To put it in more spiritual terms, corporate life is about the mind with a bit of

heart. But the entrepreneurial life is about the heart with a slice of your mind. Knowing your compass of Mission and Root Belief will instill a deep conviction and a sense of certainty. It's this clarity that fires up the entrepreneurial spirit you need to succeed.

Indecisiveness. "The bold move is always the right move" is a phrase credited to several historical figures. But it also serves as an entrepreneurial mantra to counter the conditioned hesitancy and cautiousness learned in corporate life. Waiting is a tolerated necessity in big business – but if you take this habit into your entrepreneurial venture, your brand will get trapped in the valley of indecision. In the corporate world, confidence comes from competence. In your new world of being an entrepreneur, confidence comes from decisiveness. This doesn't mean being brash or foolish. It means the confidence you so yearn for is on the other side of action. Even small decisive steps are going to produce some result.

Overuse of consensus-building. In the corporate world, one must be well-versed in campaigning. No significant initiative will be successful in a corporation without internal buy-in. That requires the champion of an idea to build internal agreement and support for the given idea. This means asking people to weigh in, taking into deep consideration all parties and making concessions and revisions designed to condition an idea, usually so it is less daring and safer — just to get the consensus needed to proceed. The opposite is true in start-up entrepreneurial efforts. Taking time to build total consensus among all stakeholders is a waste of time because it keeps you from failing fast, which is the best way toward entrepreneurial progress. Secondly, you may not have assembled reliable stakeholders. Those you are turning to may or may not share your vision, your passion and your understanding of your market. This is not to say you should entrepreneur in a bubble. But consensus-building with friends, family members, the guy in HR you used to work with five years ago or an acquaintance in a similar field is at best distracting, and at worst, is counter productive and wasteful.

If you are one of these intrepid ATLs, take heart! There's much from your corporate life that will serve you well, including understanding processes and systems, building high-performing teams, and delegating and prioritizing – among bountiful others.

Just remember: what you became to make it in the corporate world must be left behind in order to make room for a new you, the real you, the brave, decisive and passionate you — the entrepreneurial you.

3 WAYS TO STRENGTHEN YOUR BRAND FOR ANY CONVERSATION

We believe and teach our clients that brands begin in conversations. In fact, we propose that you don't actually have a brand until it is fueled by conversations.

This runs counter (as most of our ideas do) to the prevailing belief that brands begin in designing a logo or with a marketing campaign or with settling on your offerings. Nope.

It's actually much more nuanced and difficult to craft a meaningful, rich conversation than to approve a logo or hire a marketing manager. That's why most times leaders avoid really understanding their brand.

But why should you care? Because a deeper, more impactful discussion about your brand — and your beliefs, and the value it presents — will translate into a stronger connection between you and the humans who will see value in what you are offering the world and offer to pay you that value.

To begin creating a rich seedbed for deeper brand conversations, here are three suggestions from us:

Deal with your insecurities. If you have hesitation and find yourself ill-at-ease about aspects of why you exist as a company or what your main objective is or what you are offering to the world, these must be dealt with before any conversations. Do not use conversations to "feel out" offerings or to help you decide why you exist in the world. Go internal first, so that your external brand voice is cohesive, and on this foundation of truth, inspires trust. Key question: What feels shaky about your brand?

Don't project. Just as in personal conversations, we humans tend to project our biases, views and perceptions on the other person to whom we are speaking. In marketing, brands tend to project onto audiences what they think the audience needs. They make assumptions, pre-prosecute their case on shifty information and/or use persuasion tactics to get their point across. Instead of projecting, share your brand's beliefs and values. This enriches the conversation and puts you in position to listen and ask personalized questions. Key question: What questions do I need to ask of my audience and how can I best listen?

Embrace your anomaly. Most established brands want to be perceived as different without actually being different! Leaders have been trained to blend in, don't offend, make nice — all of which produce the most expensive branding strategy: **boredom.** We posit that whatever makes you an anomaly can make you a brand. Weird is good, not bad! Weird is an experience that is memorable. When you can speak to your anomalous nature and explain why it expresses something true about your brand, it invites others to join you. Key question: What makes my brand most weird?

None of these areas can be delegated to your marketing team or ad agency. As the leader, it's on you to do the deep work necessary to become a brand. This takes an investment in an inner journey – with yourself, your leadership team and your culture. The payoff is this: less pretense means more brand equity. More brand equity means greater reach, more influence and better conversations.

DON'T WAIT FOR THE WORLD TO TELL YOU ABOUT YOUR BRAND

Stop waiting for the world to tell you what your brand is.

It's never going to happen.

We are so reactionary and definitive today. *He is this, she is that.* Put a label on it and be done with it. (That's what marketing is, right? Wrong.)

Humans are obsessed with mass appeal. And way too eager to have other people define their value, which leads to squishy messages, dilution of value and worst of all — sameness.

Sameness sucks.

Sameness will kill you, and your spirit and your brand. We're all swirling around and drowning in the sea of sameness.

You know what's always more interesting than sameness? Being human. Diverse, real, raw, messy, winning, failing, learning, growing.

But most leaders are afraid to be human.

At the root of this reactionary, be-what-you-need-to-be, polished-and-coiffed mindset is insecurity — a prevailing mindset that you have to appear a certain way to support your business model. This robs you of your identity and self-worth as a leader — and it attracts people who will exploit this artificiality. This also produces more insecurity because it causes paranoia and it repeatedly incites leaders to cast about for the "right" slogan, buzzwords, or pitch.

Another root cause of this mindset is fear.

Fear creates the mental framework that being your true self will somehow harm your business model. That you might offend someone. Or leave someone out. None of that really matters because it's all a smoke-and-mirrors trick of the ego – causing you to stay in a scarcity and reactive mode.

Your brand is NOT a reaction to your business model, your employees or your competitors.

But it will be until you dig in and make it something different, something more real. Something based on what you actually believe instead of what you think the market wants to hear.

Your brand is how others experience what you believe.

In our work, we guide our clients to go inward. To shift from reaction to introspection. Why does my brand exist in the world? What are we offering that's truly different? How can we create amazing experiences?

We're not going to sugarcoat this: This is hard work. It makes our clients uncomfortable at first. It's scary. It makes you confront calcified fears. It causes you to challenge systemic beliefs.

But what are you doing as an entrepreneur if you are not being brave? Come on, now.

The payoff is worth it. The payoff is a brand for a lifetime.

Instead of chasing one-liners and talking points, you get to focus on sharing your passion and purpose with the world via a clear, heart-based message.

Instead of expensive campaigns and ad buys, you will have a consistent digital presence with compelling, story-based content. Instead of manipulation, persuasion and discounts, you will create products and experiences that people love.

We urge you to move forward bravely with this promise: large tribes of people who think like you are waiting for you. They are waiting to embrace your message, to work for you, to buy your products and services.

But you will never find them by pretending to be something you are not.

Beginning to show the world your true self is the beginning of becoming a brand.

5 SIGNS A BUSINESS OWNER HAS SHOPKEEPER SYNDROME

There comes a point in the leadership of every privately held company when the owner is forced to relinquish a healthy amount of control in order for the company to grow – or continue controlling everything and stagnate.

When business owners decide not to let go, they often become afflicted by what we call "Shopkeeper Syndrome." Shopkeepers wash the windows, count the till, measure the drapes, serve the customers, hire the help, and write the marketing—in other words, they run every aspect of their businesses. This is often necessitated by the lack of available resources during a business's growth phase but becomes a leadership habit as the company stabilizes and achieves significant profitability.

This all-too-common condition is rooted in the owner's insecurity in his or her ability to retain control as the organization grows. Shopkeeper Syndrome sufferers are often self-made and believe that holding on to once-successful strategies from the past is the best method for future development. They're scared of what they don't know—and terrified to admit it. At the same time, they take on a level of arrogance fed by their past successes.

Shopkeeper Syndrome is characterized by five key traits:

1. They believe tactics trump strategy. The most common errant behavior we see in marketing and branding—by far—is excessive focus on tactics and very little focus on strategy. Invariably, our conversations with those afflicted by Shopkeeper Syndrome suggest applying the mantra, "Strategy first, tactics second."

Unfortunately, most of the afflicted will not relent from their obsession with tactics. In fact, they seem to relish swiftly shifting between them, believing that once they find the magical tactic it will unlock a rush of inbound leads or viral hits.

Additional symptoms include: obsession with slogans and jingles, hiring SEO "gurus," copying gimmicks from their competitors, and taking advice from "samples of one" or random strangers.

2. They are always the smartest people in the room— and they're keeping it that way. Those suffering from Shopkeeper Syndrome are very insulated from people who think critically and tell them the truth. This includes both their staff and their business friendships. This deluded state causes them to feel they have the upper hand or the most experience. They tend to ask loaded questions, have preloaded responses, and are dismissive of facts and data. Our advice, "Trust your talent," usually falls on deaf ears because they think they are the only talent.

3. They have an outdated and static knowledge set and keep returning to it. At some point, these owners acquired a skill or knowledge base they believe caused their businesses to grow. This base becomes the center of all decision-making, even if it hasn't been supplemented by new information and ideas for years—or decades. When it comes to acquiring knowledge, the afflicted tend to read business books that focus on fixing other people and not themselves.

When they attend trade shows or conferences, they do so to scope out competitors, to be recognized by others in the industry, or to indulge in other forms of distraction.

When we try to adjust thinking in this arena by encouraging education about current trends such as social mobile, millennials and customer experience, the afflicted resist by saying, "That doesn't apply to my industry."

4. They have little or no talent bench. Often related to trait number 2, these business owners tend to hire people who are great at doing what they are told, doing the tasks the owner does not want to do, and/or doing what the owner can't do. Their lens of talent is focused around technical skills, not a critical mindset.

They're obsessed with leadership, but they don't truly want to develop leaders. They see no real need to develop talent because there is no one who can achieve their standards, yet they continually question why there are no other leaders. When someone talented leaves the company, they deem the person ill-suited for the role.

When we ask about the future of their businesses, we're often met with discomfort and the claim that we instead need to focus on what's going on right now.

5. They take a high-involvement, high-urgency approach to every project. The previous four traits are all culminated and amplified in this trait. When employees complain about lack of strategy, poor communication, being too hands-on, lack of clarity, inconsistent direction, and overreacting to the "next opportunity," trait number 5 is the trait they are talking about. It leads to employee and vendor fatigue, innovation stagnation, and a sloppy customer experience because the people responsible for those three areas are never fully free to own them. In fact, due to this trait, no one else in the organization is fully free to own anything.

When we confront owners with the plea, "Let it go," they often counter with, "If I don't do this right now, it'll never get done."

Do people with Shopkeeper Syndrome ever recover? There can be periods of fewer symptoms, depending on the company's balance sheet, pressure from influencers, or short-term bursts of strategic enlightenment. But for true change to occur, a healthy dose of self-awareness must be prescribed. The afflicted must become aware they've fallen into the Shopkeeper Syndrome cycle.

For those who can recognize and be accountable for their behavior, and who understand the frustration and inefficiencies these habits are creating, change is possible. But they must consistently remain open to change and find a way to trust the future of their company to people beyond themselves. It's a tall order.

To start, we recommend a tough love and brutally honest intervention—beginning by sending them this book.

5 FEARS THAT STOP YOU FROM BEING A 21ST CENTURY BRAND

In a group workshop, we were asked the primary reason leaders don't opt-in to becoming a 21st century brand.

Our answer caused audible gasps from our audience: **FEAR.**

If you are a leader over 40, you have likely reached your role or status through carefully crafted career moves; positioning yourself for the next opportunity. You've invested in your leadership development, nurtured relationships, made the right choices and produced results. So here you are in present day with all of this experience and investment — and a rising uncertainty on how to apply it in the 21st century era of business.

People may call it by different names, but behind this uncertainty is plain old fear. The best way to deal with fear is to bring it into the light. Like a vampire, by shining a light on your fear, you usually vaporize it or cause it to shrink into a non-threatening amusement.

So, let's shine a light on the top five fears you may be dealing with:

1.   **Fear of Expression:** This is the top fear by far. Many leaders over 40 have been conditioned to keep "work at work and home at home." This strict compartmentalization no longer exists in the 21st century. Compartmentalization is a relic of the pioneer and industrial ages. This fear locks down the ability to fully maximize social media, content creation and even daily conversations. The irony is this deep-seeded fear can only be overcome through expressing! So, say what needs to be said and ask what needs to be asked. Be bold! Don't wait for bravery to be a feeling – make it an action.

2.   **Fear of Rejection:** Fear of rejection is directly tied to a fear of expression. "What if they don't like what I have to say?" is what our clients usually ask. If you are speaking from the heart and someone you respect doesn't like what you have to say, then it's a learning opportunity to broaden thinking and a chance to have a lively discussion. If the person who does not like what you say is someone you don't respect, then why does their opinion matter? One method to battle this fear is to stay rooted in your intention and in your area of expertise. In short, don't brand around things you don't believe in or don't know enough about.

3.   **Fear of Damaging Your Reputation:** "What if I offend the boss or a customer?" is a common concern. Similar to the fear of rejection, this fear is born of an excessive focus on a near-perfect image. Whether you are an entrepreneurial leader or a corporate leader, you

have learned not to do things that could damage how people see you. But leadership is not about being popular — it's about being a trailblazer and innovating in new territory. Just like other leadership decisions you've made, applying a blend of common sense and courage will get you past this fear.

4. **Fear of a Lack of ROI:** "Is it worth the time it takes?" How do you know the time it will take until you've tried to do it? Whether you are working on a personal brand or corporate brand, there is an investment. Just like in agriculture, fitness and relationships, brands don't just happen without some nurturing. The key is to be consistent: consistently putting out meaningful content and being consistently interesting as a brand. Consistency gives your brand much higher "findability" and works when you are not actually working on it. And remember this: the content you don't create and ideas you don't share are far more expensive.

5. **Fear of Having your Ideas Stolen.** If your ideas are stolen, will you stop sharing them? Artists deal with this all of the time. They deal with having their songs illegally downloaded or their art copied from the web — but they know it doesn't make their art any less worthy. In fact, it's evidence of their power and influence. By sharing consistently and bravely, you will own the real estate of your ideas. In short, be so good and so consistent that they can never catch up to you!

Confidence leads to competence. What translates your 20th century equity to 21st century value is wisdom, new thinking and new leadership habits. When you believe in your own awesomeness, you will know your own value and you know how to apply this value in this brave new world. And the fear that was holding you back will become as relevant as the Blackberry you used to own.

WHY SADNESS, STUBBORNNESS & STALENESS STICK AROUND

The most stubborn remnant of 20th century thinking is that you can move people by moving their brains. And that messaging is merely an intellectual exercise.

It's not true. Not scientifically speaking, not realistically speaking, not spiritually speaking.

And yet, so many leaders remain determined to show that analytical case building will incite action. That just one more white paper, one more research project and one more committee to answer the question, "What is our message?" will finally cause the masses to rise up and make your brand famous.

Rather than replay this record ad nauseum, we began to ponder why this dead-wrong thinking still exists. And how frustrating it must be for modern-thinking directors of marketing to deal with it on a daily basis.

So why? Why is this still a thing?

To get ahead, many leaders committed their careers to the worldview that everything can be explained and justified intellectually. When *Time Magazine* declared in 1966 that

"God is Dead," scores of leaders believed it. They readily embraced the idea that behavior is just a series of levers to pull. They believed the most important takeaway from the 1963 Milgram experiments was that obedience to authority would work as a strategy in business. They became Gordon Gecko or Blake (Glengarry Glen Ross) devotees, even though both are works of fiction.

Since that era, most of these types of leaders have now retired. Yet their disciples remain in three current leadership archetypes:

> **Up In Their Head:** For the most part, Up in Their Head leaders are well-intentioned. They're just too damn smart for their own good sometimes. They feel things for people, but do not apply feelings to ideas. They love to think, and think, and think — and then think some more. UTH leaders can be reached by reminding them of their heart and pointing out that their heart is the driving force of decision-making. If they still don't believe you, you can show them the boatload of science that now exists proving decisions are made with the pre-verbal, visual and emotional center of the brain and then justified by the left brain. That should give them something to think about.

> **Filled with Dread:** Continually confronted with too much change, too fast, and too soon, intellectual arguments are the safest place for them to go. They are quick to point out that back in the early 1990s, one time with one campaign, they made an intellectual argument that sort of worked. They have likely read every book they can find on persuasion and motivation

and some variation of "Ten Tips for Getting People to Do Stuff They Don't Want To Do." The passive audience that was unaware they were being manipulated really does not exist anymore, except during political campaigns. The easiest way for them to deal with their own dread is to pass it on to you.

Spiritually Dead: The dark truth is that people like this should not be in places of leadership. They kill brands, cultures and houseplants. And they have a propensity for bad hair and pantsuits. We try to have empathy for them, we really do. But we mostly have empathy for the people who work for them. We want to send a "Wake-The-Hell-Up" card to the leader and a "Hang In There" card to their people and their customers. Being Spiritually Dead is the result of emotional and spiritual detachment and the retention of power via status quo. The most malicious aspect of SD leaders is their view that people are simply company assets and should be treated as such.

Thankfully, most of us do not fall into any of these categories. But we likely come into near or far contact with them on a regular basis. So how do we deal?

- Become well-read on the science of decision-making, how habits form and how real change happens.
- Understand the movements begun by Ghandi, Martin Luther King, Jr., Buddha and Jesus were not fueled by intellectual arguments, but by love.
- Arm yourself with quiet and challenging questions such as, "How do you know that's true?" "What do you mean by that?" "Who has that worked for lately?"

- Don't become them no matter what beverage they bring you from the bar or how tasty they say the Kool-Aid is.
- Fight their lack of soul with your soul on fire. Be unapologetic in your desire to speak from the heart to the hearts of others.
- Reject and reject again their attempts to minimize, rebuke and trample on others' dreams.
- Be a bliss burr in their saddle of sadness.

And if they want you out, then fight like hell and stir up trouble. If you lose, exit with grace, knowing the war is always more important than the battle.

Then go work for an opt-in leader or lead an opt-in organization and go be you.

AMOR FATI AND YOUR BRAND

As humans we love to quantify. Predict. Determine. Forecast.

Throughout these cycles, chaos followed order, as it always does.

In today's environment, we find ourselves moving through chaos and corruption with big forces like the internet, mobile, social change, and the rise of the largest generation since the boomers, the millennials, essentially holding up these systems of order and shattering them.

Many business owners and marketers still apply a type of systems thinking to the new world out of habit, conditioning or a desire to control.

"Let's do more market research."

"Who is our target market?"

"What's the right marketing mix?"

This, and many dated ideas of marketing, are relics of the old system of order. Yet they remain idols small business owners and marketers supplicate before in the hope of creating some order and security.

But we can't bring order out of order.

Order can only come out of disorder.

So what's a business owner or marketer to do?

The German philosopher Friedrich Nietzsche succinctly summarizes our view on this matter: Amor Fati

Which loosely translates from the original Latin to "Fall in love with the uncertainty." This means accepting the uncertainty with, dare we say, faith. Faith that if you push back against old systems, do the right things, infuse soul and wisdom in to your business, then order will return ... for awhile.

We say that you turn into the unpredictability and harness it. Make it a source of energy.

So where is this primary source of disorder?

The world? Some governing body? Other people?

No. Closer.

It's us. You. Me. We.

We as humans are made up of systems, as well as chaos. We are equal parts set structure and fluid form. Probably literally. This chaos comes in all forms. Our thoughts, our emotions and our endeavors.

In a business ecosystem, with plenty of chaotic acreage to bring order to, our system-obsessed mind tends to go nuts. We apply model after structure after system. And models are useful, but models in and of themselves, are flawed and will never trump chaos. And chaos will eventually be ordered. For a while. Of course, there's not a lot of certainty in business. Ask Payless Shoes or Sears or Kodak or Myspace or Blackberry or Blockbuster Video or Yahoo. Certainty is temporary.

The marketing you are doing today to attract leads likely will not work tomorrow. And making marketing all about one repeatable model and directing your marketing department to be ROI-obsessed order takers may lead you down a path to short-term order, but as conditions shift or roadblocks arise or efficacy fades, chaos is sure to follow.

What if instead, your marketing team were thinkers — as well as doers? What if they were strategically minded *and* action-oriented? Unless you don't want that. In that case, you may prefer to be the type of leader with all the ideas, and all the delusions of order.

We're certain of this ...

As a brave leader, you will step into the chaos. You will be able to acknowledge you are part of the chaos. And when you do, some order will begin to emerge. You will have learned that how you lead is your brand. You will know that carefully nurtured word-of-mouth is infinitely more valuable than paid advertising. You will have built systems to listen to the humans who touch your brand. You will have learned to speak truth as a counter to the torrent of well-crafted marketing BS. You will see a tribe of loyal human beings form around you.

You will see that people are drawn to your authenticity and these connections — more than just leads generated through pay per click or Facebook ads — present markedly more value and significantly bigger opportunities.

You won't be the first to boldly walk into the chaos. You can look to models like Yvon Chouinard, Sara Blakely, Elon Musk, LeBron James – and the thousands of yet-to-be-famous entrepreneurs, thought leaders, creators and makers.

We caution you of this: don't worship them and don't follow them as an ever-loving formula.

Simply let them be what they are – a source of inspiration for you to embrace chaos in your own way.

SECTION 3:
New World Marketing

MARKET AS YOU WOULD LIKE TO BE MARKETED TO

In our world, the most egregious violators of the Golden Rule are marketers.

By in large, they do not market unto others as they would like to be marketed unto.

Sadly, the marketing industry supports this disconnection between humanity and marketing.

Way too many marketers go for tactics that use the hammers of coercion, scarcity, and intrusive, repetitive exposure to market their businesses. These tactics are typically based on rapidly evoking fear, lust and envy as motivation for a sale.

Even sadder still, far too often business folks see no problem with these tactics. Unless, of course, they are the target of said tactics themselves.

As Hugh MacLeod illustrates, "If you talked to people the way advertising talks to people, they'd punch you in the face."

Here are a few additional, less obvious Golden-Rule-breaking tactics:

- **Interrupting** – inserting oneself uninvited into the mind or conversation, the entire model of advertising is based on interruption

- **Manipulating** – playing on the primal fear of missing out

- **Over-explaining** – inciting insecurity about one's own value

- **Using clinical-speak** – speaking in sterile, soul-less language, using doldrum visuals and bland experiences

- **Being pushy** – We also refer to this as blunt force trauma marketing, which culminates in generating a cult-like obsession to recruit people

However, marketers who embrace the Golden Rule typically follow a few best practices. In addition to doing the exact opposite of the above list, they utilize timeless principles, such as focusing on relationships, creating compelling experiences, telling true stories and making art with their brands.

Following the Golden Rule means replacing persuasion with invitation, replacing FUD (fear, uncertainty, doubt) with love, replacing selling features with creating an experience, ceasing managing perception with simply telling the truth.

Brands that excel in following the Golden Rule in marketing include Nike, Southwest, Apple, Subaru, Volvo and Intercontinental Hotels. These brands view marketing as an extension of their mission, culture and story — not as an external construct. They are not afraid to express what they feel, see and believe in with their brand.

They have a deep understanding of who they are as a brand and how they want to show up in the world. And because they are connected to their own humanity, they are able to speak to the hearts of their respective audiences.

This is why we emphasize going inward in our work of intrinsic branding. In order to live the Golden Rule, you must be rooted in who you are. You have to be bold enough to take an inward journey to elucidate the foundational elements of you — your beliefs, your standards, your mission.

THE MAGIC IS IN THE MESSAGE

As a child, magic is an accepted part of the world.

Yet as adults, magic becomes something that "doesn't exist." (Until we head off to Disneyland or DisneyWorld and throw ourselves full bore into the idea of magic once again). We eschew magic, yet we embrace the idea of magic wands.

We seek them out in our diet, in our physique, with our parenting, in the quality of our skin or the thickness of our hair.

In our Root Sessions™ and workshops, we say there is no magic wand in marketing. This means marketing is no longer a silver bullet for a toxic culture, poor customer experience and shoddy products.

But there is still magic in marketing …

And it's found in the message.

A compelling message has always been magic. A well-crafted message opens new places in the mind. It enters the soul. It quickens the heart. From "Follow me" to "I have a dream" to "Tear down this wall," a message driven by conviction changes the world.

The main issue is that most brands don't think of message this way. They still view message as a cheesy slogan, a witty one-liner, or a cute tagline — often delivered via the battering ram of advertising and the waterboarding of sales pitches.

Here are three simple tips for ensuring your message is magic and not mundane:

1. **Speak from and to the heart.** We ask our clients "What does your heart want to say to the world?" This is your message. It requires leaders to go inward to consider this deep question. This moves you away from two things that kill the magic: 1) trying to make an intellectual argument and 2) delivering a message based on what you think people want to hear.

2. **Meld your message with design.** Dream about your message until you feel confident creating art with it. Infusing beauty transforms your message into art. Art inspires both the soul and the mind, draws the attention of your audience and makes your message stand out. Blending message and art creates a sensory experience that subconsciously attracts people to your brand.

3. **Be consistently dedicated to your message.** This sounds extremely basic. But when you dedicatedly and heartfully deliver your message to the people who matter to you — in life, in business, something magical happens. It starts deeper conversations. It leaves people wondering and longing to know more. It suspends you above others. It begins a deep discovery process. A

word of warning: don't pursue consistency at the expense of conviction. Stay rooted in the meaning of your message as you practice this consistency.

Most of all, and if you do none of these things, just stay open to seeing the magic in what you do. Start by considering what part of your work is easy for you. We tend to dismiss what we are best at — and not appreciate the magic of our own talent and how we magically apply it.

Finally, a challenge for you …

Revisit the message you are sharing with the world as your brand. As you examine your foundations of your brand with these fresh ideas, can you feel the magic in your heart and bones? Beyond that, if your message is complex, boring and non-emotional, you don't have a message. If it is simple, unexpected and emotional, you do.

YOU DON'T NEED A MARKETING AGENCY

Small business owners are in a bit of a conundrum when it comes to marketing. You can either do it yourself or bring in a marketing agency.

Let's be real. Doing marketing yourself is not an option. Even if you enjoy it, there's too much. Contemporary branding and marketing are not something you do in the seams and creases of running a business.

A marketing agency, the one-stop shop of your dreams that only charges you a minimal monthly fee and immediately produces quality results across every single platform, doesn't exist either. Marketing agencies must fulfill too many roles and accrue too many overhead costs to be all things to all clients. That's why many of them are now specializing.

Finally, you may not be able to hire a full-time internal marketing executor. And you certainly don't have time nor energy to manage a bunch of freelancers.

There is a third way, which we practice and have instituted for our clients. A hybrid of coaching and accountability, we establish a brand and marketing foundation that centers around who you really are, why you do what you do and what type of marketing you enjoy the most. Then we coach you to take the first steps at implementing it and living the brand. As the brand becomes more clearly formed and intrinsic branding becomes a practice you and your leadership team engage in regularly, we help our clients train or find and onboard a full or part-time marketing coordinator who can take the accountability role for regular outbound brand and marketing – and storytelling.

In our model, we focus on teaching our clients four principles:

1. **Strategy first, tactics second.** It's so tempting to think that changing your logo or updating your website or trying the newest marketing fad will help produce results. But here's the hard truth: If your foundation isn't solid and level, then your house is going to be unstable at best. In this wobbly state, marketing tactics are unpredictable or are likely to crack. Further, when you get the strategy right, you can drive the cost out of marketing execution.

2. **Put your mission at the center of your brand.** By "your mission," we mean *your* mission. You, the owner and leader. Not a mission statement, but the drive in your soul that burns to build something. When you put the mission at the center of your brand and communicate it with a heart-based message, you trigger attraction and spur word-of-mouth. You are no longer using marketing to pitch goods and services. You are using marketing to invite people to your mission.

3.   **Get the language right.** Branding is ultimately a word-of-mouth practice, so we must be in agreement on what the words are. Not on a functional level, but on a soulful level. We take the time to meaningfully wire mission to emotion to specific words that precisely articulate the change you are creating in the world. This is language that stops people in their tracks, that leads to deep conversations, that, in seconds, converts the curious to the engaged.

4.   **Your brand strategy and business model must be aligned.** When not properly tended to, brand and business model tend to drift apart. This puts you in the position of branding something that's not real and/or doesn't support your revenue goals. It's like having one foot in two different boats. Many small business owners unconsciously deal with tactical bias; a check-box approach to marketing where if the task is done then you've marketed. Not true. Marketing is producing results, and results come from strategy, message and differentiation.

Marketing isn't the actual problem. You are. You've built your business by being a problem solver, which has served you well! Congrats!

But here's the deal, friend, marketing is not a problem to solve.

It's a mystery to unlock, a method that unfolds, a practice and not something one does alone.

HOW TO REALLY BE IN CHARGE
OF MARKETING

There's this paradox about being responsible for the marketing of an organization: You are "in charge" of the brand and at the same time, you are *not* in charge of the brand — *at all*.

Being in charge means you are expected to come up with, organize and execute every marketing objective of the organization. Even in small, simple organizations, there is nothing simple about tackling this complex task. It requires a ton of planning, a lot of clarity around the audience, consistent execution, total confidence in the message and help and buy-in from team members who may or may not be inclined to support your efforts. But you're tackling those challenges every day and overcoming many of them like a boss.

Not really being "in charge" means, in many cases, the people "in charge" of the brand are out in the market, in front of your audience, talking to influencers, saying and doing things you may or may not be aware of. New messages are being tested, brand promises are being made, new initiatives are being formulated — all without your knowledge. So consistency becomes a challenge, only boosting the amount of complexity you are managing.

Then, when these well-meaning leaders get back to the office and regroup with you, they have a boatload of new ideas for you to implement.

Yowza!

Just staying in alignment with your leadership team can feel like a full-time job in and of itself.

So how does one actually, truly stay "in charge" of the brand?

Here's the hard truth: you set a clear strategy and direction and then you learn how to say no.

Here are three specific competencies to begin to practice:

1.   **A-B-S. Always Build your Bench Strength**. With today's freelance/side-gig world, there's rarely a need to blow all of your marketing budget on bringing in an ad agency. But you do need to make sure you have a vetted circle of resources you can trust. Do they understand contemporary branding and marketing? Are they self-directed? Are they energy positive to work with? Once you've established these criteria, we recommend two providers for every role. This distributes the risk and also keeps them grateful for your business. Part of this bench strength are resources that specifically strengthen you – from self-care practices to hiring a coach.

2.   **Be your business's Central Intelligence Agency.** Whenever possible, be proactive about gathering and distributing information. It is so much

better to bring information to your boss rather than to react to his/her requests. This begins with curating a list of content sources and data points aligned with the business and the brand. Using a tool like Feedly allows you to track, tag and share selected content on business trends, competitors, social issues that affect the business. For data points, use a simple spreadsheet to track no more than three key performance indicators (KPIs). Then bring this with you to meetings with your boss as a powerful tool for leading the conversation about results and performance.

3. **Communicate daily with your leaders.** Do not wait for your monthly marketing confab with the leadership team to share what is going on in your neck of the woods. You need to assume and assess the thoughts and ideas of the leadership are changing daily. But don't panic; just talk to them regularly about their thoughts on the market and on marketing. Just because your boss's thoughts on marketing are changing daily doesn't mean you need to change your strategy with them. But you do need to be aware of these tide patterns. If you know what's going on in their mind, then you will know how to better do your job: what ideas are worth pursuing, which ones are worth re-directing and which ones deserve sincere acknowledgment and then quiet shelving.

Underlying these techniques is a crystal-clear strategy that all of the stakeholders have agreed to at one point. Once this is established, (we recommend doing an annual review of brand strategy facilitated by an objective partner focused on brand strategy, continuity and messaging), stick to it.

To remind your leadership of their commitment to it, you may even have them plant their John Hancocks at the bottom of your marketing plan, once it has been established for the year.

Be sure the plan has room to breathe, with opportunities for side trips and deviations. Build some buffer into it.

Our goal with any of our clients who are one-person marketing teams is to bolster their confidence and courage:

- To say a firm "no" to the ideas not part of the strategy, and explain why;
- To protect your role from becoming an order taker;
- And to ensure your job as director of marketing (or insert your title here) doesn't become daily internal crisis management for your marketing endeavors, aka director of firefighting.

IF YOU'RE NOT DIRECTING, YOU'RE DRIFTING

Directors of marketing are often mistakenly under the impression that they are actually directing marketing.

The truth is directors of marketing are often seen as marketing order-takers. They are inundated with demands. Chief among these demands are repeated calls for the three Rs: results, responses and ROI. These demands often are accompanied by being "strongly encouraged" to try the latest marketing tactic your CEO or COO heard about at the last conference they attended.

As a result, you're not really directing much. But you're getting good at asking, "Would you like fries with that?"

There's a hidden truth behind this. Like the emperor, the brand has no clothes. Everyone close to the "leaders-that-be" are afraid to speak the truth: that the brand you all love and are giving your blood, sweat and tears to, is slipping quietly into irrelevancy.

It may be happening quickly.

It may be happening a little at a time.

It may have slipped so far that you're carrying a three-font business card with a prominently displayed fax number and curiously missing any social media information.

The additional challenge is that outside of water cooler chatter, it's likely no one is talking about this. But you see it. More than that, you *feel* it. It's a general unease (and possibly rampant denial) that something is off.

So, what do you call a problem no one is willing to talk about?

We call this hidden reality Drift.

Drift is what happens when a company becomes disengaged from its root system; a set of standards and beliefs that keep cultures alive and companies growing. Like a mold problem, drift shows up in a variety of ways. Commonly, a company in drift may experience:

- Disconnection of the next generation of employees and customers from the core mission and purpose
- Trouble attracting leadership bench strength, as well as fresh front-line talent
- Wrestling with an aging customer base coupled with an inability to reach the next generation of customers
- Difficulty or inability to differentiate or assume a brand position in order to stay competitive and relevant
- Watching unexpected competition rise up and make millions taking your market share – leaving you to respond with a tepid new slogan or discount

Like your uncle in his underwear, once you see drift, you can't unsee it, so you have to do something about it.

We have a challenge for you …

1. Do you see it too?
2. Where do you see it?
3. Are you willing to be the champion of fixing it?

If so, then first try sharing what you see with your team or internal advocates. Then gather your resources, courage and make an appointment with the CEO to share the harsh reality about the brand. It's the only way to stop straying into dangerous waters and recapture your brand.

MARKETING IS A TEAM SPORT

Marketing is a little bit like a Rodney Dangerfield quote. "It can't get no respect."

Everybody in the business wants great marketing and basically nobody wants to do great marketing. This is fueled by an Industrial Age bias in many leaders that marketing still follows a direct, linear path. That there's a straight line between Product A and Audience B.

Leaders want marketing to be simple. They want it to be 100% effective, all the time, they want it to be cheap, and they want it to make them look good — overnight. Oh, and they want little to no part in it.

That's not asking for much, right?

Sure, many of these ideas have been further reinforced by the marketing industry, which has become awash with snake oil salespeople and false promises, pie-in-the-sky ROI projections and flavor-of-the-month marketing tactics.

But still. What other part of business is held to these criteria?

Do leaders expect sales to be 100% effective all the time?

Do they anticipate their accounting will be cheap?

Think their internal software will make them look good overnight?

Do they think improvements in automation will produce immediate ROI?

No.

Yet, if we had a dollar for every time marketing has been taken to the whipping post and flogged simply for being imperfect, we'd be rich.

And it's time for other parts of the business to take more responsibility for marketing, just like they would with a tech decision, an accounting system or a sales team.

The most successful marketing requires the engagement of the entire organization, especially the leadership team.

Strong marketing depends on clarity around mission, message, category, differentiators and customer experience. Those should not and cannot be uncovered or determined by the director of marketing alone. It is up to leaders to be accountable for providing a strong set of marketing ingredients to create a masterful dish that will ultimately grow the brand and business.

Have you as a leader worked with your team to give them this foundation?

Have you collaborated and empowered your director of marketing to think strategically about marketing? Once that is done, are you ready to go hands-off as your director of marketing implements, runs experiments and refines the marketing approach?

We recognize that marketing has a heightened level of expectation – especially if your company is in growth mode. In order to meet the revenue goals set forth as part of the growth strategy, marketing needs to perform at a high level.

However, this often leads to an attitude from leaders that if marketing doesn't produce to their level of expectation, then something is wrong with the marketing. This doesn't take into account a lack of clarity around the aforementioned mission, message, category, differentiators, customer experience – all of which have a direct impact on the efficacy of marketing.

This pressure for marketing to perform also can lead to steroidal-like practices: using manipulative messages or tactics just to drive the numbers. Unfortunately, way too many marketers succumb to this pressure in the face of panicked "we need leads!" or "we need deals!"

If you are a director of marketing, you need to master three things to push back against the inherent biases many leaders have about marketing:

- **Demand and earn a seat at the strategy table**. Don't let other leaders relegate you to the kiddie table. You are a leader. You get strategy. You have ideas. They deserve to be heard.

- **Become a thought leader.** Most internal marketers get immersed in the workload of their role. But investing in your own brand as a marketing thought leader will pay dividends as you position yourself internally as an expert, not an order-taker. Advocate for your own learning opportunities as well. Ask to attend conferences, take courses and join a mastermind.

- **Report back.** There is a tendency among directors of marketing to hoard information. This is understandably spurred by the consistently dubious attitude toward marketing's worthiness and perception as a "cost

143

center." Fight that tendency. Share your resounding successes (with metrics attached) and your lackluster experiences (and bring that data, too) with your leadership team. Let them know what you learned and how you will move forward from here.

Marketing cannot begin to sing until everyone in the organization understands their part and how the harmony of it comes together. This must be a group effort.

That's the only way it will get any respect.

5 WAYS YOUR EGO MAKES YOU A TERRIBLE MARKETER

Your ego has served you well in building your business. (We define ego as the mind part of you, the one who is constantly building logical arguments for or against everything you do).

It has provided drive and relentlessness over those long weeks, months and years and given you fortitude for all the highs and the lows involved in constructing this business of yours. Your ego gave you a database for all of your knowledge and expertise so you could make decisive decisions. It set in place the high standards you have for yourself and your employees.

There's nothing wrong with your ego. Except … it's likely making you a terrible marketer by creating blindspots that hurt your branding and marketing. These blindspots are caused by an over-emphasis on linear thinking and aggression – two common traits of being overbooked and overwhelmed.

[We acknowledge that calling you a terrible marketer might bruise your ego. Keep reading!]

So, take a pause, go to your heart and consider these five ways your ego is making your organization less than awesome at marketing:

1.   **Website malaise** – You think of your website too much like you think of your office furniture. "We paid $50,000 for this thing in 2005! It's good enough … and my customers don't look at my website anyway." Oh, so not true! But this doesn't really dawn on you until you are confronted with the fact that your customers are moving to competitors because of their better-looking websites (in addition to word-of-mouth recommendations, their better collateral materials and their message and brand cohesiveness). And when you realize the superstar you were recruiting backed away when she saw your company website and got the clear impression your organization is way out of date. To you, these incidents may seem to be gross injustices because you are so committed to the idea your website has very little to do with the success of your business. But that. Is. Dead. Wrong.

2.   **Pre-judging** – With experience and success comes a blindspot of "that won't work for me." Whether it's changing your culture to be more attractive to millennials, trying new kinds of marketing technology or changing up your marketing language to be more human, you often pre-judge the effectiveness of new ideas. This creates a "slow to hire, fast to fire" mindset for outside marketing advice, a continual bias against trying new things and unreasonable expectations about how marketing should still work.

One specific example is pre-judging how long a marketing, branding or well-defined digital campaign should take or its perceived value. The bottom line is: trust your experts and keep an open mind about new strategies, asking questions about the mechanics of these strategies and how others have implemented them.

3.   **Not listening** – Listening might have been a skill you honed as a less experienced entrepreneur or leader. It probably helped you greatly. But now that you've made it through the recession, the real estate collapse, and all the changes to business regulations over the last decade, you may have stopped listening. There's a lot of noise out there, we acknowledge. But that noise might have caused you to stop listening to your contemporaries, to the rising leaders in your organization and to those you have hired to provide a professional service to your business. Time to resurrect that early skill and consider opportunities to listen as a chance to recoup your beginner's mind.

4.   **Measuring before doing** – Obsession with tactics is a sign of insecurity in a leader. To deal with this insecurity, many leaders often go quickly to math before making a decision. They want to see endless sets of demographics, case studies, competitor analysis, benchmarking tables, web traffic stats — prior to any strategic execution. While they help inform your decisions, these "proofs" may really be designed to make you feel you're making a foolproof decision. In overly focusing on them, you are likely completely

disregarding the one thing that built your business: your instinct. Your gut has given you the hard-earned advantage of almost always knowing more than focus groups or analysts. Sure, you need to measure investments in marketing, but do that in combination with the ideas your gut says "go" to.

5. **A logo is branding** – "We already have a logo … and we like it," say blinded leaders when the topic of a brand re-introduction comes up. But a logo — whether brand-spanking new or outdated by decades — does not a brand make. A brand today is made up more of the experience — the experience of learning more about the brand, the experience of becoming a customer of the brand, and the employee experience of the brand's culture. Most of all, a brand is a reflection of what's in your heart as a leader. It is a monument to what you believe.

So, what's the opposite of ego? We believe it is your set of beliefs. When you go beneath the bias of your mind, you will find your heart. And in your heart is a set of beliefs that are all the reasons you started this business to begin with. It is why you have been kind to your employees, focused on customers, produced quality products and services and been a part of your community.

So, go back there. Go to that place, where there is no ego, only your brand and clear vision.

5 WAYS TO CONVINCE YOUR BOSS TO BUILD A BETTER BRAND

Has your boss started asking you questions that make you feel uncomfortable? Like "What is a tweet?" and "Where does a brand come from?"

If so, it's probably time to have "The Talk."

You're ready for this. Yes, you were hired to manage marketing, but you know you need to build a brand.

To ratchet up the pressure, the marketing director is often suddenly seen in a whole new light — as responsible for saving the business! Minus one necessary element — the founders' buy-in on what needs to be done to make this happen. We know firsthand how frustrating it is to be all tactics and no strategy, to be a marketing order taker for the latest shiny idea, and to feel the heat when a haphazard initiative goes sideways.

As modern-minded marketing directors, you do understand the importance of building a strong brand — not just extinguishing marketing fires. You just want the authority to be strategic not just tactical. You only need to be empowered by your boss to do so but may not know how to make a case for building a brand.

Gulp.

How to bridge this gap?

Here are five tips on how to have "the talk" with your boss about owning the brand:

1. **Make it about standards.** A values-driven owner will have a set of standards about excellence, perception and reputation. We believe that a brand is a monument to what a leader believes. Rather than try to tell him what needs to be done, show him how elements of his current brand don't live up to his standards.

2. **Attach to a business initiative.** To be respected as strategic thinkers, marketing directors need to align all marketing activities with the overall business strategy. For example, if a strategic objective is to grow a new line of business with younger consumers, the marketing team should be researching data, providing messaging and leading all outbound activities related to this strategy. During the talk, be sure to make the connection between your activities and the bottom-line result.

3. **Show them hard data.** While your boss might find it mildly amusing to hear you wax philosophical about the latest marketing and branding trends, she's going to *react* once she sees facts. One of the simplest ways to do this is a survey of customers and employees. In this survey, look for qualitative data

about how people *feel* about the brand. For example, one great question to ask is, "What do you love about us?" This converts feelings and perceptions to data to make your case.

4.   **Show them competitors.** Careful with this one, friends. It can quickly turn from a pile of pine needles to a forest fire! The key is asking him what he likes about what a competitor is doing, then do your research on how you envision your brand executing a similar idea in a much better way. In particular, show how your competitors are bridging their past with their future, how other owners are using new tools to generate leads and how your industry peers are being empowered.

5.   **Appeal to their ego.** A little psychological jujitsu comes in handy now and again. In this case, you are making an appeal to their sensitivity about sustaining their business, building their legacy as a leader and fulfilling their role in your development. It's all about them. You want her brand to be bad-ass, because she is a badass. She deserves to be famous. Ask that she anoint you the brand crusader and declare your readiness for battle.

Even with these tips, we know how hard these convos can be. So, come prepared, take three deep breaths before entering and say a prayer. And know when the boss says "yes," the real work (and fun) begins. Now, you'll have the freedom to build your own leadership and bad-ass marketing skills.

WHAT TO DO WHEN MARKETING IS A DIRTY WORD

We've recently been working with a Fortune 50 company to help them communicate a critical business strategy that required some sensitivity and intentional language related to a change of service.

After we presented our simple, clear, heart-based messaging with which to communicate BOTH internally and externally, we received an interesting comment.

"My reaction is: sounds like ... marketing," said one professional in our group, spitting out the last word as if it had soiled his mouth.

We don't really blame that guy for feeling that way. Marketing has painfully earned its negative reputations. Marketing language is too often used like a bad Tinder pick-up line and not a warm, alluring invitation to get to know someone better.

Marketing by its purest nature is a form of intimacy. It is the language of love, not the language of temporary romance or a long-term relationship gone stale. Real marketing is not a flashy come-on or the mundane activity that you negotiate over. It is part of the daily rhythm of a relationship between your brand and the people it touches.

You used marketing to woo people to begin a relationship with you and become your customers. Once they become customers, you stop marketing to them and start managing them. Instead of continuing to woo them with love language, you send them legalese about the end of a contract or a notice of a policy change. Or maybe worst of all, you send them a three-page ratings-based survey! Would you ever say after an intimate moment, "On a scale of 1-10, how was that for you?" Of course not!

So here are some specific tips you can use to keep the magic alive with your customers with some provocative, intimate language:

- Instead of sending out traditional satisfaction surveys, simply ask them questions like "Are you happy?" or "What can we do to make your life better?" Not only will this give you a deeper connection with your customers, it will also provide tons of useful ideas.

- Instead of talking about what you want them to do, start thinking about the conditions they face, then figure out if you have anything to improve those conditions. If the answer is yes, directly tell them about it — starting by relating to how they must be feeling.

- Offer your current customers better deals, new products, free stuff before you offer these to new customers. It has been proven over and over again that customer retention has a much, much higher ROI than customer acquisition.

- Call them by their names. You have a database of their names. Use it every chance you get! Hearing one's name has a powerful impact. In a recent study by a human behavioral company we worked with, they found the brain was most impacted when subjects saw or heard their own name.

If you want to keep the magic alive in this relationship (which keeps them attached to your brand, and an active brand advocate), think of your communication with them as a way to express your love, concern and appreciation for all they are. If you read communication copy that you would not dare utter to your partner, do not send it to your customers.

Bottom-line: stop taking conversations with your customers for granted. Stop treating them as an accessory to your business model and start treating them like true partners. Spice it up.

MARKETERS WHO HATE MARKETING

While working with a client recently, she delighted us with the following statement:

"I love working with you because I hate traditional marketing," she intoned, her green-gold eyes sparkling as she leaned in to emphasize each word.

What made this especially delicious was that she is the head of marketing for her organization!

"Us too!" we answered, both veterans of branding and marketing on both the agency and client side.

While both endearing and amusing, it also reveals a bit of gallows humor. After all, when your job is marketing, then hating the stuff you are asked to do should be cause for alarm. The mess that is a lot of marketing today is from two sides: 1) executives who treat their marketing team like 20th century order-takers and 2) heads of marketing who don't speak up and say "no."

Three pervasive 20th century marketing habits that just don't seem to go away are:

1. **Linear thinking**: In a recent meeting, someone proclaimed that marketing is simply matching what we do with what the "target market" needs without any attention to heartfelt message. She vehemently insisted if you add A (what you do) to B (target market needs), you always get C (profits rolling through the door). We listened, grimaced and gently explained no audience wishes to be targeted and no market is anxiously sitting waiting to receive some sort of marketing call to action for an offer. Linear thinking is most often found in left-brain messages or sloganeering – which don't work in the spherical world we live in of social, stories and being actual humans.

2. **Slogans + Taglines**: Speaking of slogans … what are the slogans for Apple, Whole Foods, Google, Starbucks or other contemporary brands? They don't have one because they don't need one. Yet the idea that a slogan or tagline will solve a lack (of awareness, clarity, results) seems to stick around begging for relevance like your cousin Troy's mullet. And just like your cousin's mullet, a slogan no longer makes you cool. Knowing what your brand stands for and believes in makes you cool.

3. **Paying for Attention:** As Andy Sernovitz once said, "Advertising is the price you pay for being boring." Yet for every "how do we get our message in front of people" and "how do we get our story out" is a herd of media buyers waiting to take your money and pretend you are interesting. If paying for attention worked, Sears would still be in business. We are not

saying advertising does not work — we *are* saying being boring does not work. Having no message doesn't work. What works is being interesting at the root level. What works is being brave enough to look inward to your beliefs and translate them through a message that speaks to people's hearts.

If our client's comment made you laugh, good. Now, pause and consider. Have you taken ownership, either as a leader or a marketing exec, to, at the very least, push back against these ideas? Have you introduced another way of achieving the marketing goals to your leadership? Have you educated your leadership about beliefs-based branding? Have you fought back against naysayers that claim that heart-based branding is "frou frou" or "touchy feely"?

Why not? It just might save your brand. And your job.

5 COMMON MYTHS CEOS BELIEVE ABOUT BRANDING

If you are a senior leader, you have fought through multiple recessions, market fluctuations and dealt with flavor-of-the-month marketing initiatives. So, you may view "branding" as the latest buzzword. As veteran marketers, we don't blame you. However, branding is much older, much deeper and more business-centric than you may have been led to believe.

Because of this perspective on branding, you may be supporting some mythologies that do not serve you or the best interests of your organization. In our conversations with leaders we've determined there are five common myths stopping a leader's progress in this very fractured, competitive, information-saturated and meaning-starved marketplace.

MYTH NO. 1: Marketing is a magic wand. Marketing does not fix a damaged brand, a dysfunctional culture or an unprofitable business model. In fact, in the fishbowl of the modern economy, marketing that is out of sync with reality actually amplifies brand gaps, increases distrust and produces more apathy. At best, it makes an organization look tone deaf in the marketplace. At worst, it makes a leader look like a phony. Internally, magic wand thinking about marketing creates skepticism and cynicism and further erodes the frontline's trust in executives and the direction of the organization. Finally, magic wand marketing does not fix bad math.

MYTH NO. 2: Slogans are messages. Slogans are a relic of the glory days of traditional media (TV, print and radio). Despite this era being long gone, too many CEOs think "if we just had a new/better slogan" sales would increase. The amount of time and money spent chasing the perfect slogan is staggering and puts a business even further behind. In the modern economy, slogans are either ignored, inherently distrusted or outright ridiculed. Instead of sloganeering, focus instead on the message you want to share, not the sound byte that you package it in. The message begins in your heart as the leader.

MYTH NO. 3: Ad spend correlates to business growth. If ad spend dictated brand success, then Google, Apple, Amazon and next gen power brands like The Honest Co., Zappos and Tesla would all be top spenders in advertising. But they aren't. We're not saying stop spending money on advertising, especially when it comes to targeted advertising on social platforms, SERPs, native ads, digital campaigns and immediate calls to action. These modern methods reinforce a message and/or drive short-term results. But the era of using traditional advertising to build a brand is over.

MYTH NO. 4: Internal culture and branding are separate. The surest way to have a brand failure and waste a bunch of capital is by trying to rebrand in a vacuum — removed from the reality of the culture of the organization. In the 20th century, you could use snappy ad campaigns to cover up poor working conditions, low morale and bad leadership behavior. With social media, sites like Glassdoor.com and your competition using their culture as a key differentiator, you need to view culture and branding as one initiative. And remember, how you lead is your brand.

MYTH NO. 5: The marketing director's job is marketing. Marketing is not a singular role in a modern organization. It's not about marketing mix, ad design, tactical punch lists or the four Ps. Marketing is the amplification of a message, which is a role for every person in the organization. Business decisions cannot be made separately from branding decisions. Marketing directors are not order-takers for other executives' business initiatives. Nor are they wielders of the previously mentioned marketing magic wand. They live the brand in the most public way and should represent, adjust to and inform the leadership about the marketplace, trends and the humans who touch the brand. The CEO may be the face of the brand, but the marketing director is the eyes and ears.

The end of the advertising age has given birth to the age of branding. But in many ways, this is a return to timeless ideas based on core beliefs, business common sense and organizations rooted in a unified pursuit. This requires leaders eager to bust through myths and harness the power of truth to become a 21st century brand.

THE LIE THAT STOPS YOU FROM BEING A BRAND

Being different is no bueno.

Of course, you don't consciously think that! But that's what your mind is often trained to think — especially if you are over 35. Most of us who fall into the "over 35" category came of age in the era of fitting in — reinforced during our formative career years. Wear the right outfits, say the right things, don't speak up too often or share too many of your own ideas were the hallmarks of this mentality. And whatever you do, don't talk about your beliefs at work, we believed.

These biases are so hardwired into you that you fail to realize how they are keeping you — and your brand — from fully becoming all it can be. If you are a senior leader or a small business owner, this "fitting in" bias is affecting your brand more than you realize. The biggest risk is that the natural state of your brand is BORING. Being boring is a business' largest hidden expense.

Here are some additional risks of buying into being like everyone else:

Fitting in is keeping you from standing out. The whole point of branding is differentiation. Not crass, self-aggrandizing differentiation, but truly owning what makes you different. If you buy into the "fitting in" bias, you are just another oat in the bowl of oatmeal. And no matter how much you bust your ass, your work isn't seen nor appreciated by your peers, your employees or your customers.

You're losing value. Nothing dilutes value like insecurity. The ego loves insecurity and feeds on it. So when you have a "fitting in" bias, you tend to only see your value through the lens of how others perceive you. It is likely you are far more valuable, more powerful and have more impact than you realize. But if you don't own your power, value and potential, you are an opera singer who is awesome at singing in the car but who will never make it to the stage.

Stagnation without representation. Fitting in robs you of your right to explore your true identity as a brand, thus stealing your sovereignty. You essentially surrender to an identity crisis and leave your brand to be defined by others, which nobody is interested in doing of their own volition. No one is waiting in bated anticipation for you to define your brand for them. Without exploring your own differentiators, your brand stagnates, blending into all the shades of beige already available.

Instead of running these risks, why not do something different today and begin the becoming of your brand?

Here are 3 practices to start the process:

1.   **Accept that you are different.** There is absolutely nothing about fitting in that puts you at a competitive advantage in marketing or branding. The good stuff is on the inside. Find what makes you weird. Love what makes you funky. Own your own awesomeness. Practice: Make a list of the five things that make you (personally) feel different. Some of these things might trigger fear, but behind them is the true treasure of insight and differentiation. This list will contain most of the essential ingredients for becoming a brand.

2.   **Tune in and speak from the heart.** Get rid of the filtering mentality that stops you from sharing what you really think and feel. Begin in your inner circle. Cut the crap and the surface talk. Craft messages born of your own beliefs. Then watch what happens. Practice: To speak from the heart, you must first listen to your heart. Take 5 minutes a day (we use our iPhone timers to set the time), take three deep breaths and ask yourself, "Where am I at today?" Tune into the feelings that rise. Breathe. When you're done, take some brief notes on how you felt. A 2012 study from the UCLA Laboratory of Neuro Imaging found that people who meditate regularly improve their decision-making, ability to process information, form memories and improve attention.

3.   **Start a conversation.** Open up your mind and heart to allow others to engage in a more than passing

manner. It's almost impossible to fit in when you make an unusual or unexpected observation, which is exactly what we want. Practice: Observe something meaningful in the moment that speaks to you deeply and then share that observation with someone — a stranger, a barista, a colleague you don't usually engage on that level. Observe how they react. Most people crave real, meaningful interaction. They will see you in an entirely different light if you're the catalyst for a fulfilling conversation.

CONCLUSION

"Every great brand is a spiritual experience."

This is our Root Belief, and one that has been tested over the course of the five years since we formed. It's been challenged, provoked, dismissed, questioned, yet still holds every ounce of truth today as it did then. This is the ultimate mark of a true Root Belief – that it can be placed in storms, hurricanes, typhoons of debate, dissent and destiny and emerge stronger than ever.

In late 2014, when we started putting pen to paper with our ideas and perspectives on modern branding, we felt like defiers. Scratch that, we were defiers. No one was talking about the beliefs we knew to be true – the importance of a brand beginning within the leader's beliefs the requirement to be radically different and having the courage to say no to predominant and extrinsic branding tactics. Spirituality and business were two words that were rarely paired together.

Thinking back to some of our earliest conversations, our ideas were either fully embraced or fully rejected. We either attracted or repelled, and there was little middle ground. Our earliest followers and clients were also defiantly driven, mostly solo entrepreneurs individually motivated to make a difference in their industry, while dually frustrated with the status quo.

When we began working on this book, we wondered if in revisiting some of our earlier content, would our nascent ideas still feel relevant?

We couldn't have known it at the time, but the world was on the cusp of an intellectual, spiritual and energetic shift that would pave the way even further for our work. Millennials using their newfound leadership skills to bring more emotional intelligence into the workplace. Long-standing institutions breaking down and crumbling. Technology providing more transparency. Customers with high standards and even higher B.S. detectors. And the list goes on. All of the above have contributed to the marketplace being ready for our ideas of going inward as the first act of branding.

Perhaps the most rewarding part of our journey thusfar has been seeing clients take many of the principles in this book and transform themselves and their organizations. Our client, Stream Logistics, was a prime example of this. Operating in the logistics industry where change is slow, the two young founders, Carson Holmquist and Chad Patton, learned how to turn inward, articulate their individual missions and share their Root Belief with the world.

They didn't stop there. They turned what they learned into a strategic competency of their business. Essentially, intrinsic branding became the primary driver of their marketing, which has helped push their brand forward, and impacted how they attracted talent and rewarded and motivated their people. They reoriented their team meetings to center around expression of their beliefs and standards. They spoke to their clients differently, and began having more meaningful conversations. They shared their message whenever they had the opportunity, from their new website and marketing materials to the art on their walls. Today, Stream Logistics has a bottom line they are proud of, but more importantly, a team that feels like they're a part of something great.

Speaking of stale industries, our work has most resonated here. Our message attracts clients in finance, tech, logistics and any other area that's crying out for something different. Within the staleness, there are individuals or small companies desperate to see change and willing to be the ones to initiate it. Defiers.

We hope this book sparked something within you. Maybe something defiant. Maybe something spiritual. Maybe something immensely practical. Whether a defier, a curious marketer or just an individual who knows there has to be a better way to lead, we invite you to revisit this book. The ideas here are timeless, rooted in brain science and soul, practical and proven. But most of all, they center around leading from a place of undeniable truth: your own heart.

ACKNOWLEDGMENTS

Both of us practice gratitude on a daily basis, and there is so much to be grateful for when it comes to producing a book. We are extremely grateful to Jennifer Lawhead, our Root + River Chief of Story, who edited, helped craft the introduction and conclusion, prepared the text and who coached us through the process of publication. We are so grateful for your attention and care with this dream of ours. We are blessed and grateful to have our intrepid Chief of Staff Cat Weise, who always encourages our efforts, sees around corners and reminds us to take care of ourselves. Thank you for always being there for us!

Many thanks to Anthony Ferrera from Obvious for the beautiful cover design and layout.

Thanks to Bill Soccorsy, Anne Klink and Michelle Tennis for reading the manuscript and providing your input.

Thank you to all our amazing clients and partners for the inspiration and motivation to write this book. You gave us the fuel we needed to bring Root + River, and these ideas, to life, and made it possible to share them.

Emily is particularly grateful to the late Bill J. Bonnstetter, who hired her to write her first book and whose mentorship changed her life, providing encouragement and support to take action toward bigger dreams, like this book.

Justin is especially thankful for Larry Anderson who was an early friend, supporter and mentor. Larry provided Justin unwavering support and a platform to test his ideas and believe in his gifts.